Dedications

"We All We Got... Family is Everything"

First and Foremost, "I do this by the Grace of God, not to over-glorify life and death witnessed during this struggle". Although I was sentenced to do time, I would never allow the time to do me. In the name of Jesus, thank you Lord for this opportunity to set aside my craft for others.

This book is dedicated, to the people who always felt I would never amount to anything. Grandma, if you could see me now; you would be proud of the talent that came from living that street life! You would be proud that though every time I fell to the bad circumstances, I was man enough to get up.

Mama, I know you see me because you haven't left my side yet, and although they've knocked me they ain't stopped me. Love you!

To my son, Rayshawn Dupree, it's hard looking for the maturity that I should've shown before everything brought me

to this. Yet I'm not perfect and when things go wrong, that doesn't mean that life is over. I love you my guy, I hope you're out and about reading who yo pops has become.

Beverly Coleman, Evonne Teal, and the rest of the family who cried when they sent me away; here's something to smile about.

R.I.P. Deshawn Dupree Strickland, Isaiah Joseph Strickland, Asia Renae Bell, Anthony "Stewy" Brown, Rhea Janelle Jones, Mamie Teal, Ya'shawnee Laface Vaughn, and all the homies who died in the struggle from gunplay; may the Lord keep you within his lamp and yo memories stay lit within us.

Chapter - 1 Da Need of a Baby

I was born a healthy 8bs 10 oz.'s, to a single mother of 2. My sister Sha'Day and me La 'Real. Being born in the "Villa" in '79 was like an African, being born in Harlem in the 70's (full of drugs, and to a dysfunctional family). My mom was born into a family of; hustlaz, boosters, pimps, and drug addicts. So of course, she had to fit one of the titles... and it happened to be an addict. Our bloodline could be found through the south, but we resided on the North side of Portland, Oregon.

My dad was the "hit and run" type, and if my mom had lived to be a hundred I would have never asked his identity. I grew up without knowing I had a father. A coward of a man, who's not man enough to take care of his seed nor claim him. That's not a man at all. I grew up to refer to dude as just the "Magician", because he performed a trick and then disappeared from existence.

My mom often had a cold, or so I thought. She always had the sniffles, as if she was sick and stayed with toilet paper to wipe her runny nose. I admired this woman because, other than my sister Sha'Day that was all she ever had around me… I needed Mama! When I would wake up and find her gone, I would get up with tears in my eyes searching for her. "Mama, Mama", I would say. A lot of the time I would find her in the living room, entertaining her "men friends". Tissue in one hand and a dark drink in her cup (for some reason I could never drink out of it). She would see me coming, before I rounded the corner. She would pick me up and ask, "why are you crying baby"? "Cause I didn't see you Mommy". I would say tearing up again. "Boy, I ain't gone ever leave you, you mommies baby and I love you a lot". K"? "K, Mommy".

3 years and some months later... I woke up to Mama screaming and yelling. "Get out my house now Gerald". "I'm calling the police"! I heard Mama say. "Bitch, you ain't calling nobody"! "I told you, I didn't touch yo little girl"! "Why is my baby bleeding, from in between her legs then, Gerald"? She's only seven years old, seven"! "Put the knife down Marie, and let's talk about this". "Talk, nigga you better get yo sick ass out my house now before I start stabbing you"! I heard scuffling, and a few seconds later the door opened then closed...

When I didn't hear my mom's voice anymore, I got out the bed to see where she was at and what happened. When I rounded the corner where she usually met me, I looked towards the kitchen and saw my sister hugging my mom's body on the floor. Something was sticking out of her chest, that looked to be a knife... She gasped for air, then reached for me as if she was talking through her dying eyes. Her hand dropped and that's when I ran to her, begging that she wake up. "Mommy, Mommy! wake up please", but she never did. Which meant the promise to never leave her baby alone, was broken from the answer of death.

Me and my sister were forced to live with our grandmother, on my mom's side Maggie Sykes. She already had a house full of heathens, grandchildren, and her own kids who came in and out the joint when they wanted. After my mother's funeral, I barely talked or communicated with people except for my sister and grandmother. I had hate within me, that could be seen from a distance.

My sister would always wake up, screaming in the middle of the night. "No, Stop"! "Sissy Sissy I'm right here it's okay", I would tell her making sure she was awake and looking at me. "I'm right here, La 'Real, yo brother"! I think she would have two separate nightmares. One where Gerald Adkins would take her innocence, and the other where he would kill our mom. Gerald was never charged for what he did to our mom, or my sister Sha'Day. When the police came the death of mom had shocked us into silence and left us unable to talk to them or replay any of the details from what we had been through.

At my grandmother's house, I had two uncles who slid in and out the spot all the time. One of my uncles was a drug lord, known in the streets as "Stonez". His real name was Stacy Sykes. Everybody knew "Stonez" from his get-down, including the Feds and the morgue. My other uncle, Steven Sykes, was a pimp who went by the name "Magnify".

He had hoes ranging from 16-60; and was so serious about his pimpin. If a hoe came short on his trap, he would beat her with a clothes hanger and shave her head bald. Every time either of them would see me, they would call me "Legend". They felt like, I would grow up with all the traits needed, in the game to excel beyond the normal hustla. I actually liked the name La 'Real because it was the name of the "Magician", who I had never met.

Sissy and I were enrolled in John Bald Elementary, she was in the second grade and me just a young preschooler. I had no problem learning, because everything was sounded out and spoken as if we were autistic children (say "hat" children). My grades were those of a focused individual, since we had so much help. That's where I met Shontay Gibson, the prettiest girl in my classroom. I met her and Jamie Powell on the same day. He was the craziest lil nigga out of all the preschoolers.

After being in Mrs. Nelson's class for a month, she asked all the kids to team up with the opposite sex as partners. Shontay had picked me to be her partner, putting together a puzzle. Out of nowhere Jamie tapped me on the shoulder. La 'Real, dats my girl. Why don't you switch partners with me? I must have looked at this nigga for all of 20 seconds, and then told him "no". She picked me, I didn't pick her. He stood there until Mrs. Nelson told him to please be seated. Ok La 'Real, we gone see at recess! Shontay grabbed my hand and told me to help her with the puzzle, so I did.

Recess came, and Jamie came with it. "What's up La 'Real"? He asked. "What you mean, what's up"? I shot back. "Do you know who I am"? He asked. "Yeah, Jamie Powell". "Well, I like to fight". I looked at him and smiled. "Me too, and I always win", I told him. "Oh, ok. Shontay ain't really my girl,

but I do like her". "That's cool man, I'm too young for a girlfriend, I only have a sister and a grandma". "Where yo mom and dad at"? He asked me, looking puzzled. "I don't have a dad and my mom got killed a few months ago".

"Why you wanna know anyways"? I spit back, getting

pissed. If you've ever seen a 4-year-old with his fists balled-up, then you know what I'm talking about". I'm sorry to hear about yo mom, I don't have a dad myself. I just wanted to know for no reason, is all. That day was how he became the best friend that anyone could ask for, and my love began for Shontay in a different fashion.

.. 10 Years Later. . . 1994

Me and Sissy was still at our grandma's house, but a lot had changed. My uncle Stonez, had been killed in a drug transaction gone bad when I was 12. My uncle Magnify was in jail on a life bid, for transporting minors across state lines. My grandma had begun talking to herself, when my uncle Stonez got killed. She had a few breakdowns which left her on a lot of medications. Sissy was 17 and the hottest thang in the school, and on the block. Yet she didn't carry herself as no tramp. In fact, she had never even had a boyfriend and was very much focused in school. We all we had still, and we was a close-nit family. We kept grandma alive and kickin. All the other grandkids left when both my uncles fell.

I was 15, in the 10th grade and the block knew me as Legend, not La 'Real. Even though I went to school, I played the streets like a chess board, hustlin. When my uncle Stonez got knocked off, nobody in the family was allowed in his room because grandma wasn't havin it. My other uncle was already gone. Locked up. Grandma had a bad nervous breakdown and went to the hospital. Sissy went with her and I stayed to guard the house.

Alone in the house and a lil nosey, I decided to go in the basement and see why we weren't allowed into this specific area. When I opened the door, it was a little breezy, but everything looked as if my uncle had left to go to the store or something. I looked and noticed, that he had more jewelry than the nigga Mr. T, and more shoe boxes than Payless in the closet.

Me being a lil nosier than usual, I looked through my uncle's stuff and discovered cash and a lot of drugs! I sat there about 10 minutes. It had to be 4 bricks of cocaine and about 80 racks in cash. Damn, I wasn't the hoodest nigga or the stupidest one, but I knew from this point I had to get my hustle on and get all this shit stashed. I wasn't even done searching everything, when I came across all that. I knew it had to be a lot more, if I looked through the rest of the room. I decided to go through the rest of my uncles shit and found 2x's more in drugs and cash.

What was a 15-year-old to do with a quarter ticket and 12 bricks? The first thing I did was grabbed 3 duffel bags and a shovel. I headed to the back yard, dug 2 and a half feet down in the dirt and put 11 bricks in the hole and buried it. I kept one brick to distribute. Inside the shed, I took apart the walls and hid $214,000 inside and kept $26,000 for my pockets. I also found a car that had been covered, under a tarp and knew what the keys in the house went to.

Uncle Stonez, had never driven this joint due to his death. It was an '84 Mustang, clean, with low mileage, fresh paint, no rips or tears and Gucci seats. When I saw the car in the garage, it took my breath away. I ran in the house, grabbed the keys, and hit the alarm which sounded a bit faint. Dis mufucka was clean. I had to touch the pedals in this joint. I cranked the engine and it came alive on the second try. Dis mufucka hummed, I had to slide to Jamie's' house in this bitch.

I pulled up to the Piedmont Plazas where Jamie, AKA Stix lived with his mom and 2 sisters... I stepped out the whip, with everybody acknowledging my existence. Damn, young blood, dat lil nigga just hopped out that whip with Gucci seats. All the females young and old was lookin at me, like I'm da King and shit. I nodded my head and made my way to my niggaz door. Before I could knock, the door jerked open. "Legend, wuz up my nig"? I know that ain't you, in that Babyface on Whip appeal status"? Stix said looking over my shoulder. I smiled at him and told him, "we have a lot to conversate about my guy". "I'm ready to take over the world at 15, you with me"? "Hell yeah, if we driving in spaceships that look like that joint, out and about speak the real".

　　We walked inside his apartment and I greeted his mom and his sisters, respectfully before going to his room where we were to speak. When his bedroom door was secure, I pulled out the $26,000 I had in my pocket and gave him 10 racks. "You ready to get money my nigga"? I asked him. "What, you hit a lick or something without me", he said looking at the money in his hands. "Nah, found this," pulling out the brick, "and some money in the basement of my grandma's house... It was my uncle Stonez". "How much you find"? "A few bricks and this cash I have on me".

(Word to the wise; no matter how close you are with a friend, never tell them all yo business!)

"Damn, my nig, you know what we can do with all that work"? "Yep, that's why I came to get my best friend, cuz he stays ready and wit the shit". "I'm Reggie my nigg". "Wait listen, the 10,000 I gave you, is for you to move yo mom into a house and out these apartments. These mufuckaz right here, is something like a goldmine my nigga". "He hugged me, "yep I'll do that my nig, I love you like a brotha for what you just done for my family". "Pay no attention to the gesture my nig, you my guy". He went and holla'd at his mom and then we left to tour the town in the whip we landed. "Today my nigga, we became blood brotha'z, nothin can ever come between us... We all We got"!

Chapter 2 - The Take Over

By now, I was known as Legend. A 10th grader with El'gwapo. Nobody knew that the straight "A" student was on the level of the Notorious "Strick Ninez", but I was on beyond the hustle. Sissy had heard through a few people, that I was arriving at spots in clothes that cost more than peoples rent; including their gas and water bills. When she caught wind of what I was doing, she called me. My phone rang twice before I picked it up, "Hellah"? I said. "Legend, where you at"? I heard my sister say on the other end. "I'm on the block, with my nigga Stix. Why wassup"? "Boy, don't be answering my questions with a question". "Remember, I'm the oldest out of us"! "You right Sissy, my bad. Where you at"? "I'm leaving the house with Yasmine and her sister Shontay". "Shontay who"?

"Boy, the same one you've had a crush on forever"! She laughed back at me. "Did she just hear you say that"? "Yeah, she heard me". She the one who told me, you got a Prince Purple 5.0, and the clothes you be wearing cost more than people's bills! "What you hiding niggah"? "Sissy, where are you guys at exactly"? "We on Interstate and Lombard, waiting for the bus to come". "Don't get on the bus ok, I'll be there in a few minutes". "Ok she said".

It had been months since my grandma's breakdown. Since then I had moved, 6 of the 12 bricks and met a cool connect in the process. They helped me put more money in the shed walls. I never touched any more of the money, since that first day that I found everything. My calculations put me close to 400 racks stashed, 2 in my pocket and 40 more in the trunk of my car.

When I pulled up, I dropped the top and Sissy went nuts! "Boy, I've seen this car following me before". "Why you ain't stop and give me a damn ride"? She said punching me in the arm". "Why am I catching the bus and you in the hottest thang on the streetz, and it really do got Gucci seats". I parked and got out. "Sissy, let me talk to you in private", I said pulling her away from the two females that she was with. "What Legend"? "I'm mad at you right now"!

I reached in my pocket and gave her the 2 racks. "Here Sissy, I want you to go to the bank on MLK and open an account in yo name". "I got over 40 thousand in my trunk for you to go to college, but you can't put it all in at once". "What"? "You heard me". "Bro, where you get all that money from, for me to go to college"? I had to tell the truth, being she was my all in a nutshell. "Sissy, when grandma went to the hospital for the breakdown, I found drugs and money in uncle

Stonez room". "How much? And don't lie, on mama". Pulling Sissy, a little closer to me, I told her. "I found 12 bricks of cocaine and almost a quarter of a ticket". "As in a 'mil ticket"? She asked. I shushed her but nodded in agreement. "What did you do with the dope"? "I've been having people sell it. "I got 40 thousand in the trunk for you". "Legend, don't be riding around with all that money on you like that, you hear me"? "Yes Sissy, I hear you". After I drop you off at the bank, I won't do it again". "Promise me then"? "I promise", I told her looking her in the eyes. "I love you Bro, and can't take nothing happening to you, "We all We got". "I hugged my older sister and told her that I loved her also and understand. She then whispered, "bro, we rich huh"? I smiled and led her back to my 5.0. "Everybody get in," I said.

The whole time I was driving, I seen Shontay looking at me in the rearview mirror. I cut the music down, to speak to Yasmine and Shontay. "How are you beautiful women doing, this fine afternoon"? Yasmine waved, but Shontay spoke, "hey La 'Real how have you been stranger"? I smiled, because she had never called me by the street name Legend. "I've been trying to live a little bit Shontay, can't complain how have you been doing"? I asked her back. "I could have been at my best, but I've been missing pieces to complete my hole".

15

We hadn't spoken in a few years. I believe since 8th grade to be exact. She moved to a better neighborhood and left behind a world of hoodlums, including me. Not to say that it was her choice, but you know" . . .We haven't talked in a while, why"? She asked, me breaking up my thoughts. "Um, I ain't really got an answer to that". "Seriously though, if you allow me the chance to acquire your phone number now, it won't be a long time again before we talk". I told her smiling into the rearview. "La 'Real, if I give you my number and you don't use it, I swear we gone have a problem"! "I'ma hit you ASAP, I promise you". "503-555-2551, it's my own line to my room, but my pager number is 503-555-2324". "I picked up my car phone while I sat at the red-light, on Ainsworth and MLK and paged her and put my numbers in her pager.

When I pulled up to the bank Shontay tapped my shoulder, "Wassup"? I said. "Do you think I can use yo phone? I don't recognize these numbers in my pager, with the code #1. I smiled and passed her my phone. She dialed and smiled, when she heard who the person was that presented himself as number #1 in her pager. Looking at me through the mirror, she said "yo promises look legit to me La 'Real". "Is that just for today or is it a permanent fixture"? "It's forever or nothing at all"! I smiled back.

When Sissy got out the car, and I see my nigga Stix get out also I didn't know, if it was because they caught on to what was going on between me and Shontay, but I watched Stix walk Sissy to the bank door with Yasmine in front of them. Sissy smiled the whole time, as if he was telling jokes or she was really enjoying his company. When Stix got back in da whip, he said "Legend, I'm in love with Sha'Day"! I looked at him with the serious look of death and said, "We all We got my nigga". My brothaz keepah type shit, til my flesh leaves my skin. If my sister ever give you the time of day, just remember she's my EVERYTHING, and to hurt her you gotta kill me. He looked at me for a second and nodded his head "4-sho my nigga".

My 12th grade year in high school was the realest, being that my focus became a lot clearer. Sissy had left the nest and gotten her on place by the college downtown. She was doing hella good and very much in love with my best friend, Stix from the playground. This relationship was awkward, being me and him were so close, but who better for her to be with than him? He's happy and so was she. I loved seeing them together because Sissy looked the happiest, I'd seen her since our mom was killed.

When I was in the 11th grade, our grandma was diagnosed with Alzheimer's. She couldn't remember anybody, or nothing else really. Me and Sissy decided to put her in the best old folk's home we could find. They took great care of our grandma and me and Sissy went to see her and talk to her a few times a week. Being that she had lost all her kids to the hands of another, made her not wanna remember the outside world and keep the rest within and in memory.

Being on the block, I picked up the craft of music and built a studio in the basement of grandma's house. I had developed a cold swagger, with the way I spit my words and phrases. A lot of people dug my style. I pushed the first mixtape at the age of 16, and I called that joint "Russian Roulette". The streets went nuts as if I was a star of some kind.

I needed a place to wash and rinse all the dirty money, that I had made from the streets. I wasn't a dumb nigga or a doe boy, seeking attention from the Feds; money didn't make me happy. It came with problems, so I kept a low profile and opened a couple of stores; such as Strick Standardz (a clothing store), My Brothaz Keepah (food and quick mart), and a record store I named Sha'Day'z after my sister.

By 1996, every teenage male who wanted to be

known joined a hood/gang. I mean everybody chose a name over all else and a lot of people lost their lives to fit in. In my clique I had; Stix, BJ, BQ, Hasko, Stink, Tank and Raw. My niggas wanted money above the hood and chose to fuck with me and the family corporation, "I Am My Brothaz Keepah/MBK'. We didn't get into much bullshit until Stink got killed. Fuck...

My nigga went into the afterhours spot, on Dekum, and must have had like 10 racks in his pockets (flamboyant). He was shooting dice and talking down to grown men like they were bitchez. "Y 'all niggaz don't know how to get money like Da Stink, seven". "Y 'all niggaz play the block, but me and my niggaz is the block seven". "I don't argue with niggaz, I play contact sports and knock shit down! (Bet 200, I hit the 9). The niggaz at the afterhours didn't care shit about what he said or was talking about. They was more focused on what he revealed while boasting.

When Stink came out the afterhours, he was well past drunk and unaware of his surroundings. He had taken a hood rat chick name Ladybug with him, who had been ran through by every nigga in the town with money. Stink arrived to his "72 Cutlass but before he could open up his car door, where he had a .45 automatic under his seat, 3 men jumped out a parked car and walked up on him and the chick: No words, all shots. He was robbed for his jewelry, money, car, and his life. Left with eight holes in his body, to talk for his stupidity of bragging. Rest in Peace Stink.

Stix took it hard about what they did to our nigga Stink and started mowing shit down everywhere. It made me step down from gettin money everywhere and start sparkin any and every chance I had. I wasn't no born killa, but when pushed; I could cremate yo flesh with da flame carried and fall asleep without a nightmare.

Chapter 3 - We Had a Meeting

Sissy was worried about me because my raps had become a part of my everyday living. She feared something would happen to me or Stix because, the streets not only watched but they talked now too.

(Snitches and informants!)

Anyways, so she called my phone while I was in class and left a message on the machine. "Legend, this is me yo sister, I want you and all of the fellas to come to my house, so we can have a sit down and come to an understanding about some things ok? "Don't be dragging boy, because it's very important". "My house, 6 p.m. love you". I couldn't take the call, but what she left was a good enough reason to be there at 6 p.m. sharp. Talking on the phone wasn't cool and it didn't sound like phone material. Stix lived with her, so I knew he would probably alert everybody else to Sissy's meeting.

Me and Shontay had become closer, after she gave me her number in the 5.0, the day Sissy found out about my get down. Her sister Yasmine had dropped out of school and began to prostitute, for a guy named Pretty Tony and no longer lived in Portland, Oregon. Her occupation was in Vegas and Hawaii. Shontay took it hard and really leaned on me for understanding and comfort. She lost her older sister to the oldest profession in the world...prostitution.

When she first started coming over, we would conversate, watch movies, and chill in my studio in the basement. The night everything changed; was during the movie. I felt her grab my hand and I ended up caressing spots I had never touched on her body. Up to this point we had only kissed and slept in the same bed bundled up.

Our 12th grade year, my sister called and left the message concerning the meet. I was getting out of class when my phone rang again, "Hellah"? "Hello La 'Real, this is Shontay"! I heard her say. "Girl, you act like I don't know yo voice or something. Wassup"? "I'm ready", she said. "Ready for what"? "Can we meet at yo grandma's house"? She asked. "Yeah, but ready for what"? "Boy, just meet me there and we will discuss it then, ok"? "Ok" Then the line went dead. Her words kept playing in my head as I jumped in my '96 Yukon... "I'm ready, I'm ready". ...Damn, what that girl mean she ready? I took the T.R.U out the deck and put that Monica/Miss Thang in, "Melody". . .

'so, play me a melody,
no matter what cha find,
something to roll to, and something to ease my mind.
Just play me a melody,

why we're chillin in yo ride,

cause I love kickin it with you, gettin it on,

ridin to the music and playing this song'

When I pulled up she was sitting on my porch, with a smile and the reflection of the sun was beaming off her beautiful features. I stepped out the whip and walked up the steps into her embrace and a deep kiss. "What was that for"? I asked with a smile on my face. "La 'Real" she moaned, "I'm ready"!

For two years we made an agreement to be friends and not engage in puppy love and poodle pumps. For us to have sex or engage deeper, the first commitment had to be school and logical love. I had only touched and rung her door bells, the night she grabbed my hand during the movie, but we didn't have sex. I only put my fingers inside of her wet pussy and explored her breast. I opened the door to my house while being caressed and touched. I stopped Shontay and pointed to the couch "sit", I said, and she did. I went to the kitchen and grabbed her a drink of iced tea and came back and gave it to her. "What's Wrong"? I asked her. "Why you think something is wrong"? "Because I want you"? "No, because it's all of a sudden, we just had movie night 2 days ago"! Well, let me tell you something La 'Real.

We have a week left in high school, and both us is graduating as promised. I've been in love with you since preschool, so it's not "all of a sudden". "Why you think, I picked you to be my puzzle partner"? She smiled… "I want you to be my first and last"

I stood up and felt her heartbeat, and it was as if a Seabiscuit was inside of her chest. She was scared and excited all at once. "Okay, you've made your point Maya Angelou". " I love you too, but we don't just pick a second and say go". Allow me, as a man to set the scene, which will be tonight. Not now, because a woman I've waited all my life for, can't be rushed into. I have to go to Sissy's house, in like an hour. Can I take care of that, and you spend the night with me after leave from there"?

"Do you even know why I picked you La 'Real"? "No, but I would love for you to tell me why Shontay". "I picked you because, any other man might have jumped me at the door; but you as a man, had to clarify the what's and why's before allowing anything to transpire. Which means you care about me, above fucking and that matters a lot"! "For the record, any woman who just allows themselves to be fucked, will remain fucked all her life! A woman may explore and seek the options as to what she wants, but a real man being in her life would like to journey beyond the body. Feelings of intercourse last a second, but respect and love for what's transpiring in the act may last the rest of yo life". She smiled, "boy, you think you Langston Hughes or something, huh"? I grabbed her and kissed her on the forehead, "nah baby, I'm just La 'Real. A Legend to the world" ...

At 6pm, we all packed up in Sissy's house. All together it was a meeting for seven of us, from my crew and Sissy made eight. Sissy walked into the garage and shut the door behind her. "Look gentlemen, or would y 'all prefer the word "niggas"? Being that's what y 'all been acting like... I know y 'all with the shit, the bidness, or whatever you wanna call it. When it comes to the Murda game and gettin money. Today is where you separate the two, ain't nobody speaking in my house before I finish, or you can leave now. "Anybody for the door"? We all looked around, and as expected nobody moved for the invitation.

"Stink is dead, and the rest of you are alive and kickin. Killing somebody else's child ain't gone bring him back, nor any of you if you get killed behind this ordeal. Now, she said walking over to me, "this is my little brother who I love more than anything in life, and regardless of all else his safety is my concern". You all are like brothers to me, except Jamie of course and I'm worried about everybody. If you gone get money, get money, and stay out the way of a pawn who's trying to be a king. "We all We got". Now, "am I my brothaz keepah"? Everybody said, "Yes I am"! "Didn't I say nobody speak til I'm done in my house"? Sissy said laughing. "Oh, before I forget, I expect clothes and gifts for this baby I have within my stomach lil bro's". We all turned to Stix, and even his mouth was hanging open...

"Yep, Mr. Jamie Powell, no more killa killa". You are about to be a daddy, "so man up"! I was shocked about the baby ordeal, but proud of my older sister. She had overcome the fear of a man and allowed one close enough to love and make a family with. "Congrats Sissy and Stix", I said. Stix yelled out, "Shit nigga, all of y 'all is the god daddies, and uncles so put the money in my hat"! "Boy, you is too funny", Sissy said and walked out the garage with Stix in tow. All the rest of us felt the meaning of Sissy's meeting, so it wasn't much left to conversate about. We left the "wanna-be", parents alone to celebrate.

Chapter 4 - The Real Shontay

I burnt off from Stix and Sissy's house to get ready for my night, with a woman I had dug since Mrs. Nelson's preschool class. The Real Shontay. I went to the Safeway on MLK to purchase $50 in canned fruits; peaches, pears, pineapples, and apricots. I also bought some flowers, balloons, cards, and food to cook. I went with steak, shrimp, mac & cheese, and broccoli. A meal cooked by yours truly.

When I got to the line, there was an ole-school female clerk smiling at me. "She must be pretty special" she said. I smiled back and agreed, "that she is, yes ma'am that she is"! "I can see it written all over yo face"! "Dang, that obvious huh"? "Yes indeed," she said. I tipped the lady an extra $20 for just knowing her shit. "Thank you", said grabbing the bags. "God bless you, and enjoy yo self, you hear"? "I will", I said leaving the store.

When I got home I went right into making the food, breaking the flowers down everywhere on the floor, cleaning the bathtub, and putting the canned fruit in it. I signed the cards and placed the balloons in various locations around the house. It was about 9:30pm, by the time I had the food in the oven on warm. I called Shontay, her phone rang for not even half a ring, "hello"? she said picking up the phone. "Hey there beautiful, are you still ready for the things you asked for"? I asked with a smile on my face.

"La 'Real, where are you now? I thought you wasn't gonna call me"? I'm at home waiting for you to arrive, and why would you think I wouldn't call you"? "I'm ready also". "Are you still ready, is what I asked you"? "Yes baby, I am ready for us and wherever tonight takes us". She purred into the phone. "Ok, I'm at home waiting for you to arrive". Did you happen to talk to Sissy today"? "No, you said that y 'all had to talk about something, so I didn't wanna disturb the groove of what y 'all had going on". "Why"? "She may have something she wanna tell you". "I'm on my way and I will call her when I get in the car, k"? "K, I'll see you when you get here".

When the phone hung up, I knew I had at least 20 minutes. I lit all the candles and turned the music low. I had to put that SWV on, because the way Coco expresses love, is how I make love fit me. As soon as "That's What I Need" came on, I heard the soft knock on the front door...

'I need someone who I can share all my dreams with, that's what I need...
'someone special who can love me just for me, that's what I need'...

I opened the door and finished the next verse.

'need someone to share my ups and downs and even through the bad times she'll always be around

Shontay's eyes dropped and what she started to say was, "did you know Sissy is having"? The rest died on her lips, when I sang that part of the song and she noticed the rose petals at her feet. "A baby"? I finished for her. "Yes, I did beautiful. May I be so kind, as to take yo coat"? I said looking at the spark in her eyes. "Yes, please do", she said with a smile and a glimmer in her eye. That showed me that she wanted to cry, from the scene around her.

She handed me her coat. The candlelight shinned from the table where we were to eat, to the fire place and the end tables. I handed her a rose, and the cards I had picked out especially for her. I walked her to the dining room table, where I grabbed the chair and gestured for her to be seated. I had used my mom's old China set that had all the plates and spoons gold plated. Her card read: "love is described as Shontay"... The rest of the card was blank. The second card read: "I believed in love, when I felt the pace of yo heartbeat, and it matched mine to a tee. Without you, my life would be empty and incomplete... I loved you at hello. La 'Real".

When I came back from getting the meal from the kitchen, I saw the tears flowing like a waterfall. I reached to the table for a napkin and wiped the tears away and kissed her eyes. "Shontay, look at me". I said, lifting her chin up to where our eyes met. "Make no mistake in thought, and always know that you were born to be my soul mate". "I'm in love with you". She nodded and cleared her throat, "La 'Real, I'm speechless... and really would like to say that "you give me butterflies".

"Thank you for these wonderful things, that you've done for me". "I'm in love with you also". I kissed her eyes instead of her mouth and gave her the food that I'd cooked. "You're welcome Queen". We ate and talked about what we wanted in life. She told me that, she wanted to be a wife and not just a girlfriend or baby's mom. She said she saved her virginity, until now because she wanted to make sure that she gave her body to someone would be part of her forever. I asked her how she knew that I'm the one to give such. She said, "because I trust you more than, I trust myself". If I'm careless, you will love me enough to correct my wrongs. In return, I asked her "what her plans for college were"? "I wanna get my bachelor's degree La 'Real", but I wanna go to college here and be with you"! "Is everything me"? I asked her. "Yes, it always has been with me". "Girl, you crazy", I said and took the plate from her hands.

"What's your plans"? She asked me. To this day, nobody knew of my business accomplishments except for Sissy and Stix. Nobody knew that I owned three successful businesses. "Shontay, I already own a lot and have a lot". I told her. "What do you mean La 'Real"? "Um...um...damn. I own... um... three stores". I said, scratching my head, and trying to think of a way to tell her what I've been doing this whole time. "What you mean you own three stores? "How you ain't rich", she shot back. I smiled, "I own Sha'Dayz the music store on Fremont; Strick Standardz the clothing store on Failing & MLK, and lastly I own My Brothaz quick mart". "Stop playing" ... she said with her voice trailing off. Dats my word. I'm telling you the truth". "La 'Real, those are known and successful stores in this town, you mean I buy all my music from yo store"? I can see her thinking about it for a second and it hits her, "Duh, Sha'Dayz, it's only your sisters name. Is there anything else that I need to know"? "I'm also the rapper that they call Legendary". "You a rapper"? She asked sarcastically. "I am". "Spit something for me then"! "Stop,

"Shontay you gone make me blush and I'm black", I said with a smile. "Babe, are you for real"? "Everything a man could want, I got at 17. ... except you"! "So, you could have picked any female to be with, huh"? "Yeah, but why select a female whose mind is local and not worldwide"? "I know what I want my destiny is to be, and who I want it to be with". "Enough with the small talk, can we take a shower together"? "Yes baby, we can".

I undressed Shontay and let her undress me. When we both got in the shower she kissed me hard, breathing into my mouth. "La 'Real, I need you so bad baby"! "Please be gentle". "Shontay, we are taking a shower together...not having sex". I told her with a grin. "Okay". I washed every part of her body and played with every part also. "Stop baby, you making me hot in places, I didn't know existed and I can't control myself". "Let's get out then".

When we got out she seemed confused, like "why he didn't try anything". I smiled reading her thoughts and grabbed her hand, leading her to the downstairs bathroom in which the door was closed shut. "Open it", I said looking at her. When she did, she gasped at the sight of it. It was lit with candles and the tub was half-full of fruit.

"La 'Real, what's" ... and it must have entered her mind, what the fruit was for because she said, "you want me to get in there"? She asked pointing to the tub. "Yes, I do Shontay". I said, helping her into the tub. I touched the speaker button and that "Xscape" came on.

'never should've kissed ya,
never made it back home,
told myself in love wouldn't fall...
would've been a pleasure,
just to know yo name,
oow look at me silly me,
I'm back in love again...
there's nothing you could tell me,

nothing I wouldn't do,

just hope that you're in love with me,

the way I'm in love with you...

do you want to,

like want to,

be in love with you, say you do'

"When we do this Shontay, I wanna taste everything on yo body and I want it to be sweet". "When I think of you, everything about you says, yes, she is the one for me". I dropped my mouth to her size 40-D breast, licked the nipple and then ran my hand in the tub to grab some of the fruit and juice, spreading it over her body. "Lay back" I whispered. When she did, I put the other breast in my mouth and hummed as if she taste the best. "I love how yo body taste baby, close yo eyes for me" I rubbed some juice on her face and licked her face up and down like a thirsty puppy, "La 'Real, mmmm", I kissed her deep while putting the fruit on her pussy lips. "Stand up"! When she stood up, I rubbed the fruit in every crevice of her body. She moaned "damn baby, it feels so good"!

"Sit on the back of the tub and open yo legs and close yo eyes"! As soon as her eyes shut, I climbed in the tub and put my tongue on her button. "Oh, shit baby," she moaned. I licked her up and down for the first few licks, then my tongue got diverse. "Oh baby, it feels so fucking good"! "It's driving me crazy"! She cried out. I went faster and heard a scream that wasn't recognizable, "Baby, baby, wait, please, what are you doing to me"? I licked and shook my head like I was saying "no". She bit her lip and got stiff. "Oh shit...shit...baby"! She moaned as her body started its first round of convulsions.

I sucked her pussy now as if it was a grapefruit. That's when she began to cum back to back in succession. "Oh baby, it won't stop"! She cried out. I stopped and took my tongue off her button and pushed my middle finger inside of her hot box. I then reached for her G-spot, I pushed my finger inside her deeper and felt the walls of her cave. She jumped, then her juices began to flow out of her pussy like a shook-up pop can before she squirted. The moans and jerks made her hyperventilate, "I can't, I can't . . . breathe...baby" ... She wheezed out in ragged breaths. I eased up on how fast I rubbed her G-Spot, then put my mouth back on her clit and sucked it like a baby's binky. Her pussy exploded like a volcano. She was having her first orgasm. She wrapped her legs around me and grabbed my head at the same time, thrusting her pussy all the way in my face and letting out a scream. "La 'Real, baby it won't stop fuck it feels so good"! "I'm cumin again baby...oh shit...shit". I was stuck with my mouth and nose in between her legs when she let go. It had to be 20-30 seconds without me breathing. My face was soakin wet from her cum. I was breathing like a track runner. She looked down at me and laughed, "Oh my god baby, yo whole face is white like Santa's beard".

I pulled her out the tub onto the floor and rubbed my dickhead on the entrance to her pussy. She had cummed so much, that she forgot about this part. When I pushed the head of my dick inside of her, she grabbed my arms. "Oh, shit baby, yo dick feel like a cucumber, it's big". I worked the head in and felt her back arch. "Can I put it all inside of you Shontay"? "Are you still ready"? She breathed as if she were having a baby and said, "yes I'm ready"! I pushed in and she tried to scoot back, but I stopped her, "La 'Real, oh La 'Real"... "Am I hurting you"? "Just do it". "I pushed all the way in and rocked the boat". "Oh baby, yes"! "It's...it's so deep in me...real deep"! "Am I hurting you Shontay"?

"Yes, but don't stop now". "It's in me deep baby and I don't wanna start over...it's starting to feel good...oh I'm finna cum so hard baby...oh shit"... She said this, and it felt as if she had peed on me. "Harder baby... I'm ready...I'm ready"! I could feel when I ripped her and knew she was ready. I took my dick out of her and told her to turn over. When I pushed my dick into her from behind she almost collapsed. "Take this dick, you wanted it". "Oh, my pussy baby, my pussy".

I got aggressive, but I didn't let up... I pushed faster and faster and when I was about to cum she yelled, "stay in me baby I wanna feel you cum in me"! I exploded inside Shontay. The first sexual encounter for both of us, and I had performed like a Champ.

(thanks to all the sex tapes I had been using to study).

Usually a nigga of my stats with loaves of bread up under me, and so young, wouldn't have taken a chance of cumin inside a female but fuck it, I'm a hood nigga and she was the love of my life. Real niggaz, make shit happen.

We both graduated with flying colors, and being she deserved something nice, I bought her the white '97 Range Rover on18's. Fresh 18 but grown. . . It had been six months since the night we got down at my house, and since then we noticed a big change. Shontay and Sissy was both pregnant. I only had sex with her one time that night, being that everything was so intense, and we were exhausted. We woke up on the bathroom floor sticky. A month had passed, and she asked me to accompany her to Planned Parenthood. The rest is history... Oh, and for the record she moved in with me.

Chapter 5 - You Musta Forgot

Me and the new daddy of a baby boy, Stix was on Albina passing out flyers, to my upcoming concert when a base head walked up to us. "Hey, is one of y 'all working"? A way of asking for dope from us. We both looked at the old nigga, because for some reason something was very familiar about him. It made the hairs on my arms stand up... Dude reminded me of somebody, but I couldn't put my finger on it.

We had a few chicks in front of us asking about the cost of tickets, when all of a sudden it came to me. Bam! "Aye youngster, you look very familiar". Who's yo people"? he asked interrupting my reverie. I lied, "I ain't even from round here homie". He then asked Stix if he had that Nick Cannon on him. "Yeah, my nigga, what's up"? he asked.

I pulled Stix to the side and told him to hit that lick and find out where the base head lives. He said okay and walked off to conduct business. "Aye," I yelled as he was walking away, "if he spending big get his number so we can hook up with him again"! The smoker smiled and said, "I like dat young nigga... he's on his hustle tough like"!

When Stix walked back up, he could see the emotions flowing through my expression. "What's up Legend"? "Why you ask me if I had my thang on me, and you got yours in the truck"? He asked looking at the expression on my face. "You look like you just seen a ghost" ...

"Alright y 'all, make sure y 'all come to the show. It's gonna be live, promise. Here's $25 a piece to hand out the rest of these flyers for us. Come on Stix, let's go. "Wassup my nig"? "You acting hella strange like... who you see"? When we got to the Tahoe I turned and looked at him directly in his eyes and asked him, "have Sissy ever discussed with you about Gerald"? "You mean the creep who touched her and killed yo mom"? "Yeah". "She told me that for years she blamed herself, for what happened to yo moms because she died trying to protect her from what the dude did to her"... "Yeah, that was just him that you sold the dope to"! "The base head dude"? he said pointing over his shoulder towards the block him and the dude had just rounded. "Yeah". Stix started beating my dashboard and yelling like a crazed animal" ...Calm down nigga! "You got his number, right"? "How much did he spend with you"? "A hundred dollars". "Yep" I said, "he should be done with that in about 20 minutes"!

I had Stix call Ol-School back, 25 minutes after we seen him. He picked up the phone on the first ring. "Aye Ol-School, you like that cream I gave you earlier", Stix asked him? "Hell, yeah boy, that shit was Rick James Fire and Desire", he said laughing at his own metaphor. "Where you say you live again, so I can drop you off a nice package. That's only if you got licks though". "Licks"? "I got so many licks that they should have called me sucker" ... "Man I live on Interstate by Overlook Park" ... "Can you meet me in the park, in about 15 minutes"? "Sure can, in the back where it's dark at"? "Perfect my nigga, I gotchu". Stix said hanging up the phone. "Dats official my nig," he said looking at me. I stopped by Fred Myers to make a phone call. I grabbed a pan and knife set, before we slid over there.

We parked around the corner from the park and walked up on the spot, Ol-School had described around in the back where it's dark. On the approach we spotted the host of our thoughts, and he spoke first. "Aye, young hustlaz, y 'all got that good soup that make a nigga wanna slap his mama"? "What's up Ol-School"? "You like a niggaz whip appeal behind dat stove, huh"? "Hell, yeah dat shit is like a first-class trip to Heaven or Hell, you feel me"? Absolutely I do my nigga, that's why I brought this for you", I said throwing him a 50 piece of that 70% pure Cain. "You don't mind if I try it right here, because I spend over a thousand dollars a month on some bullshit". "Naw I don't mind, be my guest". "Let me know what you think of the stabbing effect", I said and smiled at him.

He pulled his pipe out his pocket and loaded it with the dope. "Excuse me y 'all, no disrespect". He said as he started to hit the glass dick. "None taken", I answered back still smiling. I could see Stix was fidgeting, so I tapped him, so he could chill out. The smoke left Ol-Schools pipe, and he whistled "man, dat shit right there is stronger than the Pope's prayers". "Man, youngsta I need y 'all in my life" ... "How can I be own with y 'all"?

Just then a female strolled up on us, with a pit-bull wearing a black hoodie. She looked a little pudgy, from the baby she had a few weeks prior. She was still my older sister Sissy. "Excuse me gentlemen, can any of you tell me how I get to the regular trail in this park"? She asked looking back and forth between all three of us. This was the first time Stix had spoken since we arrived. "Ask Ol-School, he know" Stix said, pointing at the older man in the group. She walked closer to the old man, the one who had taken her innocence and killed her mom. "Excuse me sir," she said taking her hood off and getting in close proximity to him. "Do you know how I can reach the correct path in this park"? She was staring him directly in the face. "Umm ... you go down that way and ... hey, you look like" "who, Marie"? Sissy cut him off, "the woman you killed 13 years ago"? "Or the little girl, who you put yo big ass fingers in her little ass pussy, then had the audacity to try and fuck on"? "Yes, I'm her"! "Hey, wait a minute here". "I'm not who you think I am, my name is Gerald" . . . "I mean James, dey call me Ol-School" ... He stuttered out trying to back up and looking for a way to run.

Stix snuffed the nigga with a right cross and knocked him on the ground. "Shut yo bitch ass up"! Sissy's dog was at attention in case the nigga moved. "Watch him Rocko", she said. "Aye Ol-School, I know where you know me from now... you killed my mom because she found out you was molested my sister"! I pulled out the knife and handed it to Sissy and said, "you start, and I'll finish" . . .

Later that night...

This is Shawn Roberts, reporting from the fox 12 news... We are currently at the river where a body was located disfigured. It looks like an apparent homicide. The detectives are here trying to figure out why and who, would do such a thing to a human being. If you have an information regarding this ordeal, please contact crime stoppers at 503-555-9123 or the local authorities. . .Shawn Roberts reporting, fox 12 news.

Chapter 6 - A Better Man than the Magician

I was in traffic on my way from the studio I had built in the community for local rappers to record, when my phone rang. "Hellah"? I answered. "Baby, it's time"! I heard Shontay yell on the other end. "Time"? "Yes"! "Me and sissy just arrived at the hospital". "My water broke 30 minutes ago". "I won't let them touch me until you get here", she told me breathing hard. "Look Shontay, be calm baby...I'm ...umm . . . on my way" ... "Why you just now calling me"? "Baby, I called you as soon as it happened". "You must didn't have no reception in the building". "Oh, my bad sweetie". "It's okay La 'Real, can you hurry up and get here though"? "I don't feel safe, without you here by my side". "Okay babe, I'm coming now, ok"? "K". "Bye". "No, don't hang up please". "I feel better with you on the phone...it's as if you're here already". "Okay babe, what you eat today"?

"You sound like you more nervous than am... I'm okay baby, just need you"! "Girl, I ain't nervous"! I was terrified, dippin in and out of traffic like a Nascar driver. "Babe, I'm here". "I know, I can see yo truck". I could tell she was smiling by the way she said it. "Where you at"? I asked her getting out of my truck. "I'm in the doorway in a wheelchair" ... "Oh, I see you now"!

"Are you going to park yo truck"? "Fuck that truck, that's material shit. Tell sissy to come and park it or something". "La 'Real". "Huh"? "You can hang up now", she said reaching up to touch my face. "You're next to me". "Oh yeah ok bye I stuttered out and hung up the phone, and you not nervous, huh"? Shontay laughed as she led me into the hospital.

It took Shontay 12 hours to deliver us a beautiful healthy baby girl, 8lbs. 11oz's. We named her Eni'yah Marie Sykes. I wouldn't give the doctor's my daughter back, once they put her in my arms. Sissy pried her out my arms. "She mines", sissy said.

"Boy, they still got doctor stuff to do with her and you can't take her home right now anyways" ... "Oh"! "Shontay, dat boy is crazy about Ny already", sissy told Shontay. "I see, dang" she said smiling about it.

I walked out the room before caught a kidnappin charge. I went to my truck to meet my niggaz. Out of the presence of Shontay and sissy, for the first time in years I broke down and cried. I thanked Jesus for the beautiful baby and family that He had given me. Thank you, Jesus, for keeping me here to see and feel this type of happiness.

I met my sunshine on March 29th, 1998 at 3am. When I opened my eyes and lifted my head off the steering wheel, everybody was in front of my truck with smiles on their faces. "Congrats"! "Damn, I never seen the nigga cry til he had his first child". Stix said trying to clown me. "Shut up Stix," I said. "I wasn't crying, just yawned and my eyes started watering". I told him with a grin. "Yo story, yo story"! "We been right here since you first put yo head down on the steering wheel. Ain't like we gone tell Shontay and feel like you pussy for the happiness". Stix said smiling. "Boy, when Sissy had little Jamie you were sweating and acting as if you were the one pushing and shit"! "Matter fact, y 'all remember Stix being so confused that he grabbed my hand"? Everybody laughed. "I needed somebody to hold, when I seen that thang open up and the head popped out". "Yeah I bet". I grinned at him. In all, everyone who came to see my bundle of joy was Raw, Tank, BQ, Tanisha, BJ, Hasko and Kristie. We blew a few sticks of Greenday and drank a bottle of Hennessy.

My phone rang, and I answered, "Hellah"? "Boy, if you don't bring yo ass back up here and lay with me and the baby I'ma flip out!"! Shontay was yelling into the phone. "Cut dat out ma'am, I'm only outside with the family", I said trying to calm her down. "They here and ain't came to see me and the baby"? She definitely wasn't calming down. "I'ma cuss they ass out too"! "I'ma put you on speaker phone...go head", I told her once she was on speaker. "What about yo sister and niece, keepah niggas"? "Y 'all forgot who pushed"?

"La 'Real just pumped"! Raw was the first to speak, "hey sis, we all thought you may have been tired and were resting". "Resting? Hell naw! I'm sitting here feeding this hungry little girl". "Oh, we on our way up then". Raw told her. "Give us like five minutes but send the baby snatcher in". Who everybody asked at the same time? "He know who he is," she said laughing. Everybody looked at me and I lifted my shoulders as if I didn't know who she was referring to.

Everybody came upstairs to greet our first child, congratulate Shontay and see Sissy. When everyone left, the nurses took Eni'yah. I fell asleep with my head on Shontay's stomach, and her rubbing my neck. I had been pretty much out the way and off the drug scene, since the Lord gave me my beautiful daughter. Matter of fact, everybody stayed in the hustle game but me and Stix. We as men, devoted everything to the families that we created. Seeing my daughter for the first time, made me give the rest of my work to my crew, BJ, Hasko, BQ, Raw and Tank. I washed my hands of the past...

I had excelled in the drug game and knew when it was time to call it finished. At the age of 20, I hadn't had as much as a traffic ticket. No run-ins with the police and my beefin gig didn't exist unless it was on wax...

I loved music and my CD's were doing big numbers, now that I had found happiness. I was to tour with Luni Coleone, C-Bo, Water, Killa Tone and Bankroll (Portland's Finest) and a few other names who pushed the west coast after Snoop and Pac.

47

Anyways, my music didn't define my business moves. I had been a silent criminal getting money since the age of 17, but I had money that my grandkids wouldn't be able to spend before they died. (Cake)

Raw had done a drug deal with a nigga named Speakerbox, a cat from Park Village, who turned out to be a police informant. Raw didn't call my phone when he got knocked, because when I gave them the drugs, I had washed everything clean. They had enough money for a lawyer on their own if needed, plus bail money.

(When one of your homies touch a cell, you always post for his freedom, cause the heat can bring out the hoe in a nigga)

I went to the 7-11 and got me a prepaid phone and called all the family together, even though I wasn't the boss. We was all equal and I was part of the reason my click was eating. We met at a restaurant in Lake Oswego, called Eddie Ray's a low-key spot with nobody in our business. When everybody made it to the spot, I waited for the orders to be completed and then spoke.

"Aye, what they talking bout with Raw"? Hasko was the first to speak up. "I don't know bro, but I'ma send a snow bunny down there tomorrow to check him out". "Who is his lawyer, and where the Speakerbox nigga at"? "He got some dude named Ray Dupree". They say he a real good attorney and a capable black dude". BJ said. BQ cut in, "as for the Speakerbox cat I got a line on him". "A mixed bitch said he be over there all the time like". "Who the bitch bro, and what's the characteristics"? Stix asked BQ. "Dey call the bitch Barbie; she been a blade walker for years" ... "They said the nigga was trickin his dick off and throwin stacks at her", BQ told us. "You asked bout the nigga, or she just volunteered the info"? Stix wanted to know. "Nah, the bitch called herself impressing me; by mentioning a nigga who was light-weight gettin money, so she could wrap me in da web". "As if she had options", BQ laughed back at us.

"Right, use dat bitch line when you leave us and take her to a room". Stick dick in her and open her pores as well as her windpipes. "Don't ask bout the nigga directly but get the route to where his pillow lay", Tank said making it clear where his mind was at.

"Yep, gotchu Tank", BQ told him all serious now. "I would advise anybody who got something, to allow the smoke to clear, before going on about business" ... "All y 'all should be cool paper wise, and if you not then get at the Legend, I'm here". Everybody nodded and said, "We All We Got", together at the same time.

A few days later Hasko hit my dum-dum phone, and told me that Raw hadn't got caught with any work, but had made a controlled buy with the Speakerbox nigga. I gave Hasko and his family my regards and hung up the phone. "Baby, what's wrong"? Shontay asked me. "Nothing Shontay, why you ask that"? "Well because before the phone rang you were being mannish playing with my stuff, and then you just stopped and got out the bed". "As if you forgot that you made me all wet and horny". "Oh, maybe I just got ADHD"? "Not when it comes to my pussy". "Okay babe, you're right, but after I handle this call I'ma give you action at the title". I told her with a grin. She never questioned me about my street life, because one day she might have to be my alibi. "Okay baby", she said with her lips poked out as if she was pouting. "Can you hurry up please before the princess wake up"? "I wanna be nasty for King-Kong". I smiled and beat on my chest like a gorilla.

I walked out the room and went downstairs in the basement, to have my private conversation. I called BQ on the dum-dum phone and asked, "what's the diagnosis on the profile"? "Aye, Shawn I was just about to call you" ... "Just out and about in the A-town", BQ said when he picked up. "The

bitch with you right now"? "Yep, gotta dump and wiggle"!
"What's the closest park from her spot"? "Track... Mr. Burger",
he told me being discreet, so she didn't catch on to what was
happening. "How long"? "15-20, I'll have everybody there"!
"Ok, Shawn, tell everybody in Atlanta I said "Aye". Then he
broke the connection and hung up.

I came back in the room and started grabbing clothes.
Shontay turned her back on me, showing me her naked ass. "I
knew it"! she said. I kissed her mouth and told her I'd be back
ASAP. "Be careful babe", she told me as I was on my way out
the door. "Ok, I will" ...

I called everybody and had them meet me in the park, in
less than ten minutes. I was walking laps, as if I were out of
shape and needed exercise. When BQ hit the track we all
closed the gap. "What's the science my nigz"? BQ asked as
we walked up.

"You the map and you got the layout for the treasure",
Hasko told him. "Speakerbox live in the numbers, on 172nd in
a brown house". "He has a chick who stay there, two kids and
a pit-bull in the backyard" ... "The bitch say she was over there
a few days ago, and his chick and the kids are on a trip and
won't be back for 3-4 days".

"She told you all that"? Stix asked him, twisting his face

51

up. "Without a question, and she even gave me $1,500 of the niggas money"! BQ shot back. "Damn" ..., Stix said "what you do for the bitch"? "Lick her pussy and ass or something"? "Cut the crap boyee" .... "All hip game and no lip game, plus she a hoe nigga"! BQ said laughing. "So was Kesha and Tasha, but you still tongue kissed they insides". Stix clowned him. I cut in, so they would get to the business. "Fuck the small talk, who want this scalp"? "I'm with that dirt," Stix said. "Absolutely not, y 'all own a part of the damn graveyard already" Hasko said. "Am I my Brothaz keepah"? "Yes, I am". "I got this", Tank chimed in. "I'm with you on that route". "Okay, y 'all be safe and the next time we meet, let it be a family outing for everybody". "Da kids need to mingle, so let's say the water park out by Seattle in two weeks", I told them. "Yep", everybody agreed and we all said, "We all we got"!

Hi, I'm Shawn Roberts, reporting live from Fox 12 news. We are feet from a house, on 172nd and Division. Where a body has been found, apparently by the homeowner and her kids at about 3 pm this afternoon . . . The victim has not been identified by the authorities, but it's believed to be the male resident of this home. Homicide detectives are sorting through the evidence. From what I've been told, there is large number of drugs that's been found along with the body... May be a robbery attempt. If anyone has info. regarding this specific ordeal, please contact the authorities. Shawn Roberts, Fox 12 news reporting

When Hasko and Tank had made it to the house, BQ was with the Barbie chick, so she didn't suspect that he was part of the hit and gossip about it to somebody. Speakerbox heard the dog barking and walked outside to check, and see what the problem with the dog was... "Murda, why you out here barking so damn loud"? "You know we got neighbors and shit". The bushes shook and out came Tank, pointing a 40 cal. at Speakerbox. "Don't be a hero big guy, where the money at"? Speakerbox turned around, and Hasko was glued to his back like a hoodie. "Don't speak, just walk back into the house and get what this gentleman asked you for blood". Speakerbox didn't have a choice, with two men on his head, but to do what they ordered him to do... When he did, he lost his mind... "Boom"!

We all met up in Washington, near Seattle at the water park. Me and Stix were the last two to come. We drove together along with Shontay, Sissy and the kids. When we walked in, we were greeted by Raw, his girl Sasha, and they son Lil Stinky (named after the homie we had lost). There was also Tank, his girl Tanisha, and both kids Veronica and Anthony. Hasko brought Kristie and they daughter, Millie. BQ showed up with his baby mama Angie, and they three kids Ty-Ty, Leni and Day'shawnique. BJ was accompanied by his fiancé' Anjanique, and they son Lil B.J. A couple added nieces and nephews but altogether there was around 25 people.

I had called in advance and ordered nine rooms for the families, with three beds a piece. Food and expenses was on me. As far as rooms went, I spent 20k for everything but what wouldn't you do for your family?

I hugged all my dudes one by one, with a smile. I was happy that our older brother Raw, had been returned and the charges dropped. "Good looking on that gig, Legend". Raw said hugging me. "For what bro"? I asked him. "The loud box gig". "It wasn't me bro", you may just have a few Guardian Angels of some sort". I said smiling. Hasko and Tank, had not told Raw anything he just got out and didn't know... The real men behind his release, didn't seek gratification. They kept family business, family and never mentioned a word to him. What you don't know, won't hurt you. . . As long as you out and about, just enjoy the love of those who love you while you can... We had fun.

Chapter 7 - Meet Me at the Altar

Shontay enrolled in the same college that Sissy went to and graduated from, when she became pregnant a week before we left high school. She had already been accepted into Portland State University. It had been four years since she enrolled, and she was graduating with her bachelor's degree. She already had an associate degree. I was happy for her, mostly because most women; when her man has money and they live together, turn out to be couch potato bitches ... Spending money they ain't earned, bragging with an ego large as the moon. Not my Shontay, she had a vision and she stuck with it. I had rented a ballroom to throw a surprise party, after the ceremony and made sure that nobody told her about my intentions... NOBODY.

Before me and Eni'yah joined Shontay at her school, we

went to the mall and did a lil mommy shopping. I had to buy her a necklace and bracelet set. I had Eni'yah a shirt made that said, "I LOVE MY MOMMY" with a picture of Shontay on the front. I couldn't put it on her at the mall, because she kept lifting her shirt showing her stomach trying to see her mommy. "Daddy, mommy right here on me", she said pointing at the shirt. I bought Shontay a necklace and bracelet set, that ran up the bill on my black card. When we arrived, I could see Shontay, Sissy, Kristie, Angie, Anjanique, Tanisha and Sasha sitting together in one of the middle rows. I came in with a suit on, daughter in hand and all the fellas behind me. Shontay smiled, when she saw me and all my niggas. We all wore suits, with our women's name engraved over our hearts. We sat behind the women, to symbolize that we were the backbones of the family. I leaned forward and gave Shontay a kiss, and it started a chain-reaction. All my niggas did the same thing and we all giggled.

When Shontay saw Eniyah's shirt, Eniyah spoke up "look mommy! I have two mommies now"! All the females thought it was so precious and wiped tears from the corners of their eyes. I put my daughter in Stix arms and leaned forward to massage Shontay's neck. "Baby, I'm so proud of you"! She leaned back and allowed me to massage her neck, "thank you baby. "I love you", she said as was rubbing her neck. I reached in my pocket and grabbed the bracelet and necklace. "I love you too, and I would love for you to wear this gift", I said putting the necklace on her neck.

Sissy turned and lost her breath. She tapped Kristie on her shoulder "girl, that boy just put a house on her neck". Sissy told her. They made a noise "umm... umm" when they looked at her neck. Then I reached for her wrist and added the matching bracelet. "You've made it baby and I'm happy you accomplished your goals". "You stayed up, when you could have just laid around, I told her while was put the bracelet on her wrist.

Just then her mom, sister, and dad walked in and sat at the three empty seats next to us, but behind Shontay. I was still massaging her neck at this time, when Yasmine called her name "Shontay". I could feel her freeze up under my touch. "Shontay", Yasmine called again. When Shontay turned around, she saw her mom, Megan, her dad, Rodney, and her older sister Yasmine. She hadn't seen Yasmine since she was a 10th grader.

"Yasmine", she yelled out in surprise. "Hey beautiful, long time no see". Tears flooded both of their eyes and they stood up and hugged each other. "I've missed you Yasmine and I love you a lot". "I know baby", I'm here now and I will never leave you again". She said wiping her baby sisters tears away. Somebody in the rows behind us, yelled for us to sit down so they could see. When we sat, Shontay looked at me with a look of love, like I had never seen from anyone before and smiled. I grabbed Eniyah from Stix and handed her to Yasmine, an aunt that she had never met before today. I smiled back at Shontay, and she mouthed "thank you" and all the women teared up.

We sat and listened as they called the names of the graduates. We clapped at all the accomplishments, of the people who made something out of life and of themselves. Mr. Stewart, the announcer had called almost all the names when I got up under the pretense of using the restroom. I met one of the other announcers in the hallway and he gave me Shontay's degree. I smiled, and he gave me a thumb up. My stomach folded from the butterflies I was feeling, but I was most definitely ready.

When I walked back in, the lady behind the podium said, "before we announce the completion of this ceremony, can we please have La 'Real Sykes up here to speak on our last graduate's behalf". I walked past Shontay and the other family members, without even a glance. I stepped on the stage and thanked Mr. Stewart, and the other staff for allowing me this opportunity... I also thanked the audience! For the last graduate, I present to you Ms. Shontay Gibson and awarded her with her bachelor's degree, majoring in Social Science. The crowd went apes. She stood up and made her way to the stage. When she got close enough, she shook hands with and hugged the lady who introduced me. She then stopped an stood in front of me. I handed her the degree, with a 3.5 carat diamond ring wrapped around it.

I took a deep breath into the microphone and asked for the crowd to bear with me for a second... They quieted down. "Shontay," I said, bending down on one knee, and reaching for her hand; "umm, I've been in love with you since preschool, and being that you have been my every thought, can make me your everything else also"? Shontay, "will you be my wife"? I said, sliding the ring off the degree, and holding it in front of her. One of the announcers took the mic and put it up to her mouth, so she could be heard. She was crying so hard, but she managed to look at me and answer into the mic. "Yes, La 'Real, I will marry you"!

I stood up and slid the ring on her finger, which already had been sized. I kissed and hugged her and then took graduation pictures with her. The auditorium went nuts and we walked down hand in hand, to be greeted by family and friends. "This concludes our graduation ceremony, I wish the best for you all and the Mr. and Mrs. to be... We were swarmed by our friends and family.

When we got in the car, Shontay had a smile on her face and screamed, "I'm in love with a king and I'm going to be a queen! His queen"! I smiled and kissed her mouth hard. "Baby, you've been a queen. I just ain't crown you, until tonight"! "Baby, where Eni'yah go"? She asked me, looking around. "She went home with yo mom and dad". "Why"? "We going to celebrate our engagement and yo graduation". "Okay". I pushed the play button, and that Jagged Edge, "Let's Get Married" came on...

'See first of all,
I know them so-called players wouldn't tell you this,
but I'ma be real and say what's on my heart'

"Baby, where did you find my sister at"? Shontay asked me, turning down the music. I looked at her, "find yo sister at"? "Yes, you're the king of making things happen"! "Baby, it wasn't me who found her, it was Sissy". "She flew her in and furnished an apartment for her, with the rent paid for a year... I did know about it"! "The pimp dude hasn't been seen since". "Sissy, huh"? "Yep, Sissy", I said and smiled at her.

We made it to the ballroom I had rented, and it looked empty and deserted. No cars in the parking lot, but I still had a door man greet us as we got out of the car. "Hey, how y 'all doing tonight"? "Alright, thanks for asking", I said back. I reached in my pocket for a tip, to thank him for alerting the people in the ballroom that we were on the way up. "Y 'all have a great night", he said as he palmed the $20 I slipped him. "Thank you, sir". I think we will", I said laughing as we entered the elevator. I kissed Shontay and said, "I'ma beat mommy's pussy up tonight". "I'ma need that done from my husband to be... all the moves you made tonight made my pussy wet", she said smiling.

We made it off the elevator and to the ballroom door. When she grabbed the handle, the door came open and everybody from the ceremony yelled, "SURPRISE"! Shontay jumped and then punched me. She leaned close and whispered, "yeah, we might make a baby tonight... how things keep happening". "Mommy Mommy"! Eni'yah cried out running up to Shontay laughing. Everybody from the ceremony earlier was there. All our friends, family, and her fellow graduates, professors, and everyone's kids. I had posters of Shontay made and boxes of congrats, for all those who graduated. "La 'Real, yo puzzle is complete now", Shontay said. "Yes baby, it is"!

I left Shontay to mingle with her friends, sister, and classmates. I then took Eni'yah in the room, with the other kids and the hired babysitter. Later I went and met with the fellas. "Man Legend, boy that proposal you made tonight made Tay feel like a real queen", said Tank. "Man, I try, I just wanted her to know that; I respect her woman's worth and the independence it took for her to be a mom and go to school all in one", I told him. "Yeah, my nig, you just pushed the bar for us, and tonight is officially "Legend Night". "The convo's in our beds tonight will consist of all that took place. "Did you see what La 'Real did for his wife-to-be, and how he proposed"? Raw said doing his best impression of his woman's voice.

"All the women gone be giving us hints and shit", he finished with a grin. "I feel you Raw," I said. "When I was a kid, I did things of a kid's nature, now that I'm a grown man, all childish things are behind me". "Man, up my nigs, and place that ring, on the hand of yo somebody special". "We All We Got", I noticed head nods, then I told everyone to just enjoy the evening.

When we finally made it home, it was 2am. Shontay

was very excited; school was over and the fact that her sister came back, plus she had been proposed to in such a fashion... I put our daughter in her bed, my baby was passed out, as if she partied too hard. Poor baby. I kissed her on the forehead and walked out of her room. When I walked back in my room I heard faint music and the shower going, so I stripped and got in behind my queen. "Hey, you," I said grabbing her from behind. "Hey". She purred back.

"Did you enjoy yo night"? I asked her. "Baby, I don't think anything in life will match tonight's feeling... you made me whole and thank God, for his lack of mistakes". "He made us an elite team and gave us a beautiful blessing, family wise". "If yo mom had lived for this day, she would have been happy and proud of the man that you are La 'Real", she said, turning around, and caressing my jawline. I smiled, then kicked off a session that didn't end until a beautiful little girl arrived at our door at 9am. "I'm woke now", Eni'yah announced, "I'm woke now Daddy"!

Chapter 8 – A Long time Coming

In 2002, my grandma passed away. It had been a long fight to reach the gates of Heaven, but I know that she's not suffering anymore. She met with Christ, who died to amend all burdens, of Jesus. My uncle Magnify's kids came back, to see if their names were in grandma's will along with uncle Stonez' four kids. When they arrived, I gave each of them 10 thousand and uncle Stonez' jewelry... That's the least I owed them, since their dad made me the Legend. Maggie Sykes died in spirit when Gerald killed my mom but held on to her mind until uncle Stonez was ambushed. After that she started to slowly spiral down, getting worse and worse until the end came. She left the house to me and Sissy, but Sissy declined the house being that it held so many memories and nightmares. I was the sole owner.

I never had a grandfather, dad, or any other male figure in my life and yet I was the backbone of the Sykes family. We put grandma in the ground next to Stonez and my mom, I made sure all her kids names were engraved on her tombstone. She was all that her kids had ever had, "A MOTHER". In her will was some money that uncle Stonez left in her account. I gave all those proceeds to the rest of the grandkids. I sent my uncle Magnify, some pictures and money for a good attorney. He had been in jail for eleven years already, fighting to get back on appeal.

Chapter 9 - Drumline

2003 came with a bang... After New Year's, Tank and Stix was in Tanks hum-thang sitting and talking in the whip. Both watched as 3 masked men, approached them with their guns out and pointed at them. "Get the fuck out the truck now". Tank always bragged, "I'm bullet-proof in my hum-thang nigga"! "Mufuckas, fuckin with the hood president"! When Tank stepped out, they told him to give up the keys to the house. Which he did, being that this spot was an "in-and-out" house..." Y 'all niggas get in the house now", they told Tank and Stix. When they got into the house, the robbers demanded money and drugs from both. Tank told them where the safe could found. The safe contained 35k and some house deeds. They stripped them both, ran their pockets and then shot them both in the back 4 times each. Tank ended up partially paralyzed and Stix was left in a coma fighting for his life.

When I came out of the bathroom, I heard Shontay scream, "hell naw when girl"? I couldn't understand anything until she said. "Yeah, he right here... here babe". "Hellah", I said into the phone. I caught the voice and cries of Sissy but couldn't understand what she was saying. "What's wrong"? I asked her. She gasped as if she couldn't breathe, so I told her to calm down and talk to me" ...They...they...shot them! They shot them. . . Jamie and Tank" "What are you talking about Sissy"? Who shot who"? "They shot my babe and he's in a coma, they don't know if he's gone live"! "Which hospital y 'all at"? I asked her with urgency in my voice. "Emmanuel" she sobbed into the phone. "We on our way right now Sissy" ... The phone went dead in my hand. I went to the room and told Shontay, "let's go now"! She saw the look on my face, and saw me grab my 40 cal. "Baby, don't take that to the hospital".

"The police gone be everywhere, it just happened". I punched the wall and my daughter screamed. "No daddy, no"! It was the first time either of them had met Legend instead of "Daddy or La 'Real". When I realized that I was showing them, who I can be compared to who I am, I put the 40 cal up. I told Shontay to get a bigger purse, and take the .380 I had bought her, since she had a gun license. "Babe, calm down and give me the keys to the truck", she said holding out her hand. So, I gave them to her.

"While sitting in the passenger seat, my mind was running wild. "If my nigga die, on my daughter and dead mama everybody gone get it"! Who could have snuck up on Tank and Stix? Them niggas stay ready. Dis my dog from day one, my sister's hurt and Tank paralyzed... Legend, fuck da bullshit, you gone make shit happen fo yo niggas... "We All We Got", I said to myself in my head. I felt Shontay rub my neck, "calm down baby, it's gonna be ok". When we pulled up at the hospital, it was just as Shontay had predicted; police everywhere and all my niggas and other family members was outside. Females were screaming, babies crying, and niggas were cussin. "Shontay, take our daughter inside and try to find Sissy and Tanisha". She grabbed my hand and made me look at her. I told her I was okay now and then she let go of my hand. She went inside the hospital, as requested... but not without a last glance back at me.

I walked up to Hasko, Raw, BJ and BQ, "Wassup y 'all"? I asked them. When they turned to me, I could read the weather on their faces, heavy showers of rain with hail. "Who been in there"? I asked. Raw spoke up first, "I have bro, but they ain't trying to let nobody but Tanisha and Sissy in to see them"! "What it look like"? I wanted to know. "Tank just got out of surgery". "He and Stix were shot four times each, in the back", Raw told me. I looked down at the ground to prevent the tears from welling up in my eyes. . . "Tank is partially paralyze and Stix is... umm... in a coma", Raw said. Not able to meet my eyes, with his head down. "Where was they when this happened"? "In front of a lounge spot by Irvington Park," Hasko said. "Nobody know nothing bout nothing"? "Who or why"? I asked with rage in my voice. "Nah bro, nothing". I could see that Hasko was sad to give me the news, that there was no news. "Let me go in here and check on Tanisha and Sissy" ... I said hugging all my niggas before walking toward the entrance. "We out here" ... they said as I reached the door.

I walked in the hospital feeling confused. My stomach did a somersault because I just couldn't believe this shit happened. I bent the corner and my nephew lil Jamie ran up to me. "Uncle, uncle, I want my daddy! Is he gonna die"? I bent down to look him in the eye, and told him, "naw boy, yo daddy ain't gonna die"! He the strongest daddy in the world, and plus he loves you and yo mommy too much to ever leave y 'all". "Kay" lil Jamie, I said with a sniffle. I seen my sister and Tanisha and hugged them both at once. "Y 'all walk over this way with me for a minute". I led them to a corner for some privacy". "We got kids in this muthafucka and we gotta keep it together for them". "Y 'all hear me"? "Yes bro," Sissy said crying, and Tanisha nodded. "La 'Real, I just came out of there with Tank and all he keeps asking me is where is Stix"? Tanisha told me. "Do he know what happened"? I asked her. "Yeah, he said he only wanna talk to y 'all about that"! She sounded upset about it. "When can he have visitors"? "In an hour or so, the lady said" ... "Ok, tell him that we'll be in there to see him, when we are allowed to" ... "I'll do that now". "Good looking out Tanisha, are you okay"? I asked her because she was looking bad. "Yeah, I'll be fine". "Okay". I turned to Sissy and looked at her, and she reminded me of the little girl, hugging our moms dead body on the floor...

Her eyes were somewhere else. "Sissy," I called her, and it seemed like, the focus came back into her eyes. "Bro, not Jamie" I told her that she was right, "Not Jamie" ... "That man

69

is not gonna give up Sissy". "He's loved life, ever since the two of you became an item, and dying is not in this script". "Boy, why do I believe you, as if you know everything"? "Sissy, the story must go on. "We All We Got, remember"? She hugged me and wiped her face. "Do it look like I've been crying bro"? "Not at all". I lied hugging my older sister... not at all.

When we stepped back into the emergency area I could see Shontay had settled everybody down. The kids were cool and the grownups... Nobody spoke of what we were all facing, concerning Stix health and Tanks' footwork. I walked over to where Shontay sat, with our daughter lying asleep in her lap. "Hey," she said looking up at me. "Hey" ... I said back. She reached over and kissed my eyes. "They gone be fine baby, just fine", and for some reason I believed her.

The doctor made it okay for me and all the men in our family to have a 20-minute visit up in Tanks room, so we all snuck up there to talk to him and find out what had happened. When the door shut, Tank looked up and saw all of us there, he asked "where Stix at"? "He in another room bro, but he good". BQ told him. "Man, they snuck up on us so fast... we couldn't do shit"! "We gone put the pieces together my nig, I promise you". Hasko said. "I did everything they asked, and they still shot us"... Tank said with tears spilling out of his eyes. "They know its consequences my nigga". "If not, they gone find out on Stink", BQ said with anger at the top of his mind. "I don't even know why we got out the hum-thang". "It's like an armored tank". "Why wasn't I thinking"? Tank said beating himself up mentally. "Don't be too hard on yo self bro, just get well and we gone do the homework", Raw said trying to calm him down. I finally spoke up, "is there anything you can remember about these niggas"? "Yeah, it was two of them who were big, about 6'4", 250lbs and the lil one had a high-pitched voice like Smokey off Friday". "Anything else that you can think of"? I pressed him. "Yeah, they took my "We All We Got' chain, so wherever that turns up, we know who the owner is" ... "Okay bro, get you some rest and I'm going to send Tanisha back in here", I told him getting ready to leave. "Okay, tell Stix to meet me in the hallway in a few days". "Will do bro... we love you my guy".

I stayed in the hospital for a week straight with Sissy and sent Shontay home with lil Jamie and our daughter. The doctor pulled me to the side and asked if we should try to allow Stix the chance to breathe on his own without the machine. I told him that I had to check with my other family members before I could answer his question. I walked in the room where Sissy was with Stix and said, "Sissy, we need to talk". "About what"? She asked me. "The doctors wanna try and let him breathe without the machine", I informed her. "No"! What if he stops breathing"? "We have them put him back on then" ... "Why is that even necessary bro, when he's breathing now"? She asked tearing up. "To make sure he still here and not brain-dead"! "What do you think we should do"? "Dats my nigga since preschool and he always been a fighter, so I believe he gone beat this Sissy". "If he leaves you today, he knows from within that it would crush you and his son" . . . "Member when he walked you to the door at the bank that day I gave you money for college, and you smiled the whole time"? "When he came back and got in the 5.0, I told him to hurt you, he would have to kill me" . . . "So, we should say yes"? She wanted to know. "Yes, Sissy. I believe in Jamie"! "Tell the doctor yeah, but first let me go talk to Jamie".

"That's fine, go talk to him". She went in the room alone, with the man who had given her love despite the hurt she felt growing up. "Jamie, baby, you are my everything and I can't live without you" ... She grabbed his hand, "Baby, you have to come! Member you promised me a daughter and to marry me? I'm scared baby and can't raise lil Jamie by myself. He needs you! My brother hasn't left yo side and he's acting tough as if he's okay but baby, he's not! I'm not alright, I miss making love to you and screaming yo name... Shit, since you been here I forgot that I even have a pussy, yo pussy baby... Don't leave me, I promise I need you baby. "We All We Got", member"? She kissed his mouth and rubbed his eyebrow with her thumb. "I never trusted a man with my heart but you, and I pray today that you don't break it by leaving us". "I want you to be my husband Jamie".

I walked in and told her, "Sissy, it's time for them to come in here and check to see if my guy ready to return". She nodded and smiled. Whatever had taken place in that room with her and Stix, she was no longer crying. She and I both walked to the hallway and let them test fate. At 12pm they unplugged him from the machine and by 12:01pm, Stix was breathing on his own...HE WAS FIGHTING!

I hadn't been to church since my mom was alive, but me, Shontay, Sissy and everybody else went for repentance to Mount Olive. Pastor Martin spoke of a light and being in the dark tunnel. He asked if there was anybody, who wanted the light to shine in their world of darkness? I stood up and turned to my whole entourage, "we need that light" I said, and everybody stood up with me. In all, there were 20 of us who got prayed over. The preacher praised God and thanked

Jesus, and we all prayed to the lord for the safety net to cover us as a family.

Chapter 10 - Da Wakeup Call

It had been a month since the Tank and Stix ordeal. Tank had begun to feel his legs, slowly but surely but still couldn't walk without the assistance of a cane and some deep therapy. I had been up there every day, right along with the rest of the family waiting for the sign of some good news. I had just left and went home from the hospital to be with the kids and Shontay, when my phone rang. "Do you know who I am nigga", said a voice that I didn't recognize. "Who is this"? I asked starting to get mad. "The same nigga, who was gone push bark dust through yo mullet at recess"! "You must have the wrong line homie" ... "I don't comprehend yo download and don't know who this is", but it was starting to come to me.

. .

"Stix and Stonez may break my bones but lames could never mirk me"! Then it hit me... Stix "Aww, shit"! "They done woke the dead up, huh"? "When you tired, sometimes you gotta rest til you ready to wake yo game up". He said laughing. "Damn, my nigga! I'm glad Jesus know you, because you had me shook for a minute". "I just left there a few hours ago". Shontay walked into the room and asked, "why you in here yelling like you won the damn lottery"? I smiled and passed her the phone. "Hello" ... she said, not knowing what to expect. "Wassup wit my sis, and why you ain't pick me to be yo puzzle potna"? Stix asked her still laughing. "Boy, you is too funny, and I didn't pick you because who wanna put together anything with a five-year-old nut"? "We missed yo crazy ass . . . hold on", I got somebody who wanna talk to you"! Shontay told him, handing lil Jamie the phone. "Ummm...hello"? "Aunt Shontay, ain't nobody on the phone" lil Jamie said. "Say hello again and you might hear them". She told him grinning from ear to ear.

"Hello"? "What's up with you little man"? "Um, nothing", he told Stix and whispered, "who is this"? to us. We shrugged our shoulders and told him to tell us who it was? "What you been doing"? Stix asked lil Jamie. "Staying at my uncle and aunties house"! "Why"? "My daddy won't wake up, and my mommy cries a lot". He told him, tearing up. "When do you wanna go home"? "When my daddy go home, with me and my mommy"! "Do you miss yo daddy"? "Yep, and I heard he won't die because he's the strongest daddy in the world". "Who told you that"? "My uncle La 'Real told me that" ... "I am the strongest daddy in the world". "Nah-un, my daddy is Jamie"! "This is yo daddy"!

The phone dropped, and lil Jamie ran up on me and Shontay and said, "my daddy is on that phone"! He said pointing at it. "Go pick it back up," I said to my nephew. "Hello". "Daddy". "You waked up"? "Yep". "Do you still love me"? "Yes! and you tricked me daddy", he said smiling. "Daddy sorry for tricking you...put yo uncle back on boy". "Okay daddy, I love you". "I love you too".

"I'm on my way" ... I told Stix, soon as I got the phone back. "Where is Sha'Day at"? He wanted to know. "You mean she ain't up there by now"? "No, I'm alone up here". "Nigga, you ain't never alone, "We All We Got'". I told him. "Don't call her phone... I'ma hit her line and bring her with me, when come so act sleep Snow White". "Yep". I gave instructions for Shontay and the kids to leave 30 minutes after me, and to alert everybody when she was on her way to the hospital. I called Sissy, she was at Yasmine's house asleep on the couch. When I got over there, you could tell that had cried herself to sleep. "Get up Sissy" I said, shaking her by the shoulder. "Boy, don't be waking me up like that you scared me"! "I'm sorry, can you ride with me and talk to me"? I need you". "What's up bro"? "I had a nightmare". "Boy, you got a woman for that shit now...but come on, I'll listen".

We were driving, and I said, "oh, let me take these cards and balloons to Stix room and then we can ride and talk". I said pulling into the hospital. "When the last time you been up here"? "Yesterday morning...I'm starting to lose it". "You'll be okay Sissy". We got off the elevator and there wasn't a nurse, doctor, or anybody else in sight. We walked in the room and everything looked as all the other times we had been in there. Sissy walked in behind me, "ain't nobody washed his face". She said. She went in the bathroom, wet a towel, came out and began to wipe him, as she talked to him. "Baby, I'm here and I'm ready to go home and sleep good, but I refuse to go to that house without you" ... "Please come back so I won't be stressing anymore". I'm lost without you", she said, spilling tears out of her eyes. She leaned over to kiss him, first his eyes, then cheek, nose, then his mouth. When she got to his mouth, he kissed her back and held her in a hug embrace. She screamed, then looked upon a set of eyes she feared she would never see again.

"I like when you wash my face baby" ... "I dreamed about you". Stix said smiling up at her. "Don't you ever in yo life scare me like that again"! "You hear me Jamie"? She said crying hard. "I hear you baby". "I missed you Jamie". "It's okay now baby, I love you too".

"I hate you La 'Real," She said laughing. "I know Sissy, I'm glad I could shake you awake to end yo nightmare and take you to face yo reality. I love y 'all". I said, huggin both and walking out so they could have a few minutes before everybody showed up. It wasn't long until Sissy and Stix made up for the lost time. Matter of fact, they was joined at the hip; wherever she was, he was also. Tank and Tanisha walked that dead leg out during his rehabilitation, but he was left with a limp. Our females pressed up on us hard, after this ordeal. Made it to where we couldn't do complete assignments to turn the homework in... We didn't know shit but home plate.

I had a concert to do in Eugene called the 'Chronicles of a Legend', in which I shook the spot up. "I know y 'all like, when this nigga give us a dose of what he taking, huh"?... Anyways, after the show me, BQ, BJ, Hasko and Raw was walking when my phone rang, "Hellah Stickman". "What's the toss up bro"? "Shit". "Y 'all ok"? "Out and about"? I heard Stix say from the other end. "Yep wish you were here my nigga, we left the building torched call the fire department"! I told him laughing. "Yes sir, I will be at that next joint" ... "I'm off punishment now"! I laughed and asked, "what, they got halftime now"? "Hell, naw nigga". "I'm in love with the warden and for small favors I get outings, but I gotta turn myself back in". "Damn, that's heavy, but I'm glad you rockin with the best". "Yep, da world's greatest". We both laughed.

I was walking through a crowd of niggas and bitches when a female stopped and announced me to the crowd. "There go Legendary". "Aye my nigga, what's hood"? A lil bitty nigga asked me. "Legend, of course my nigga"! "Yeah, you go my nigga, me and my niggas rap too". "Yeah"? "What they call y 'all"? I asked him. "Click Clack Crew" "Aye, Legend"! I heard Stix scream into the phone that I still had pressed against my ear, "that's the voice my nigga"! "Click Clack, huh"? Spit something for a nigga then", I said to the lil nigga and then asked Stix, "what voice"? "The nigga in yo face, is he a little nigga"? Stix asked me back. At that time the little nigga started spittin:

'I spit verbal, but I may have to bury yo crown,
Hot venom in songs cuz I'm in um and still carry da town,

79

Got niggas on bloody Mary snatchin chains from da hounds,
Cats den turned poodle watch me noodle his sound,
Dogs shittin like doo-doo kickin, voodoo spittin like rounds,
R u still down? I get around for da business,
commit crime at night cuz I don't want my shadow as a
witness'

"Yeah bro," I told Stix right before the lil nigga finished.
"How many is with the nigga? Two big niggaz, huh"? "Yep".
Damn, I need that corpse". "Okay".

'I spit llamas like I'm ipkiss for da gifted and lifted they cash
loaded gas like its kerosene'

"Okay my nigga," I said into the phone, then to the lil
nigga in front of me. "I like that shit you was kickin, I can use
you on one of my tracks". "Where y 'all from"? I asked
handing Hasko the phone. "We live out here my nigga, before
you get to the freeway". "We came out here from Spokane,
Washington", BQ, Raw and BJ looked at me like, "why
Legend just lie to the nigga bout where we from". "Nigga,
y 'all can come and fuck with us and these bitches". The lil
nigga invited us. "Yep, we with that right now". "Follow the

headlights of my Range thang, I got over yonder. I told the niggas with me, "let's go", and we jumped in the truck and Hasko passed me the phone back. "Legend, what you finna do bro"? Stix asked me. "Save the map and allow the two to get they get-back"! I told him, getting hyped-up. "Yep, call me when y 'all done with that". "Yep, "I told him. "Gone", Stix said and hung up. Turned around and looked at everybody in the whip, "dats the niggas who did that to Tank and Stix"! "I knew you was on some shit when you said we from Spokane, Washington". Raw said, gritting his teeth. "Everybody get yo 40's in yo waist bands and we gone flave".

We got to the niggas house and these lil niggas had a baby mansion. We got out and it was niggas and bitches everywhere. "Wassup Legendary"? A nice Mexican and black mixed chick said. "Hey mamacita, where the drank at"? I asked her. She pointed between her legs and said, "I don't know but I got the juice"! We all laughed at the gesture and kept moving, because we knew that groupies fuck households off. We pushed towards the house and when we got in there it was a booth and the Clack nigga called me up. "Legendary, wassup my nig? What you know about this booth thang? Step in and vibe with the clack nigga". He said, gesturing for me to come inside. I stepped in and they dropped a beat, so I went in:

'Should I fall back on em or put a contract on em?
Or treat em like a parachute and pull the strap on em?
Blap on em, black sack on em...have niggas homies telling
stories pourin yack on em,
Young Shaq on em and pullin down racks on em,
and my kicks clean like I spilled Ajax on em'

Everybody yelled, and I stopped for him to punch in:

'Catch me in da blind, I'm on my Stevie Mr. Wonder time
Felta fishin hoes with Cuccumbas doin undalines,
Humor in da summa, keep a thunda for the wonda'd minds,
Clack wit da kidnap, da raps, plus got da other grinds,
jack black for the two flap sacks motha car and his brothas
shine, Clack from the gutta, blood spittin slugs like its
Columbine, Back track wit niggas plug, cuz heart tickin like its
Valentines'

I came back:

'Any coward can turn killa, but the best is born,

'Niggas spit dat rest mess til flesh get torn.

A legend for that vest stretch, first to test my garm,

In da field like da next pest, when I release my left arm,

in da corn call me Malachi, to travel high,

I seek and destroy when my paddle rise, my shadow dies'

"Damn Legendary, you gone just Zone out like that on a nigga"? "We gotta hook up my nigga". Clack said. "We can most definitely do that my nigga". "That shit you was cooking up taste good". I told him back. "Here homie, take my number". "Who house is this mufucka we in though"? I said looking around me at this big shit. "This joint me, my nigga, but my two homies over there live here too. We eatin heavy like my nigga"! "I see, I'ma check a few of these chicken heads out and probably turn a block towards the pad". "Good lookin on the house manners my nig". "No doubt, anything for the Legendary one... just don't be stranger, now that you know where I'm at". "Yep, I'ma stay on yo line". "I owe you and yo niggas for some real shit". I could see that it went right over his head. I slapped his hand and embraced him. Then turned my back on him and gathered my gorillas before left the joint already knowing my next move, treasure hunting'

When I got back to Portland I dropped everybody off to their cars and went to Stix house to tell him that he'd won the prize. "The little niggas got a baby mansion and got enough nerve to try and rap a little". I told Stix. "Fuck those niggas bro"! "Did you get the info to make a nigga famous"? "You betta know it"! "Dats what life's about, huh"? "Yep". ...

"I love the Legend in you boy". Stix was actually happy, like he just came from Cancun with a million naked chicks. The door came open and Sissy stepped in, "what's going on bro"? "Why this nigga smiling so hard"? Sissy asked looking at me, like I was up to something. "I don't know Sissy, ask him". "Boy please". "What's up Jamie"? "I'm just proud of what Legend has did with this music thing, and glad that I will be at his next show"... Aye bro, "I could be like yo hype man". "We would torch the spot"! Stix said winking. "That happy, huh"? Sissy wanted to know. "Yes babe, that happy"! "Let me find out y 'all got some hoochies or something". "It's curtains and I'ma black out on y 'all niggas"! "Cut the crap Sissy, we don't play those type of games"! I told her. "I know bro, I was just joking, dang". She said kissing my forehead. "You better had been joking, shit". "Shut up boy and hurry up with my prisoner... "He got some hole time to do"! She said winking at

Stix. "Y 'all is nasty", I said. "I don't never wanna be free". Stix said as Sissy walked off. "Give me a week bro, and I'll have the map and directions figured out". "Okay Brain, hurry up so Pinky can take over the world with you"! "Nigga, you're more nuts than Planters". I said smiling.

"I love you bro"! "Ditto my nigga. I'm on my way to see my babies. It's been a few days since I felt that hotbox". "Bye my nigga". Stix Said pushing me out the door.

When I got home, I laid with my Queen. I had missed her... Although I had been around a million different chicks, none was Shontay. Plus, I'm engaged to be married. I crept in the bed naked and ready for the body heat she provided. "Hey baby," she said from her sleep, "how was the show"? "It was okay beautiful, but I wanna entertain you"! She backed up into my stick and reached back, "Damn, I can see and feel". She laughed. "I played with my pussy today, thinking bout both of y 'all". "Both of us"? "Yes. You and that dick". "Is that right"? "Yep," she said, showing me the toy that made her sparks fly. I knocked it to the floor and kissed her deeply. "I'm ready" said. "What type of ready is this"? "Eni'yah type ready," I said putting her breast in my mouth.

"I think it's too late for that planning stuff... um... I took a test this afternoon and I'm pregnant now". She said, reaching under my pillow and handing me the EPT test. "You were supposed to find that before you found my pussy". "Here, and after you look still give me that ready dick because I'm addicted"! I turned the lamp on and looked at the test and it said positive. I smiled and put it on the night stand and kept the light on. I kissed Shontay deeply on her lips, then on her eyes, nose, neck and then inserted her peanut butter complexion nipple into my mouth. "Ahh baby, I like when you taste yo bah-bah".

I sucked harder and moaned with it. "I love when I pout, they are here to suck". "Mmm, shit, when you talk and taste it make me real real wet". I licked my way down to her beltline. "Yes baby, you know that's my spot". I opened her legs and skipped her pussy and started sucking on her inner thigh making it vibrate. She moved my head to her lava box. "Taste the icing daddy... it's so sweet"! Put my tongue in her pussy and slurped. "Put the icing on daddy's face. "Damn, yo pussy is so wet". "Blow my candles out daddy". I tongue-fucked her hole and made, my way to the bottom to blow out the lights. "I wish for this to never end". "It just started," she said with a moan. I made love to my wife-to-be, and then threw away her toy while she slept with our baby inside of her.

Shontay slept all morning, so I got up to feed my

princess, "Daddy! I want cereal"! Eni'yah told me as soon as I walked out of my bedroom. "Nope, not today. I'ma make us all breakfast! You want some eggs, sausage, hash browns and toast"? "Yep, and orange juice daddy, not milk" "Okay, no milk for my baby". "Daddy, why mommy sleeping all day"? "She tired from staying up talking to daddy all night". "Why you not sleep too"?

"I have to feed my princess and queen when they are hungry"! "You the king, huh daddy"? "Yep, and yo daddy," I said, giving her a few sausages. "I like being my daddy's princess," she said chewing her sausage and humming. "I love being the king and yo daddy". "Yep, my daddy the king". I smiled and finished the whole meal. "Princess, get daddy the orange juice out the fridge". "Okay".

"I turned the Disney show on in the living room, made a pallet with mats down and left Ny to enjoy her meal and show. I went to the bedroom, wet a towel with hot water and wrung it out so that I could wash my woman's face. I sat on the bed and she still didn't wake up. So, I wiped the drool and her whole face, seeing her honey brown eyes open. "Hey sleeping beauty". "How did you sleep"? "I didn't, I was drugged and taken advantage of". I laughed, "At least you didn't wake up on the bathroom floor all sticky" "I may need another fix when this high wear off" ... "I can still feel you in my system". "That's fine my lovely patient, but first can I feed you and our kids"? "Yes". "Here," I said handing her a plate. "Breakfast in bed". "Damn babe, you cooked and served the meal"? "Yep, my heart is at yo service". "I like being at yo hospital". "I operate and you're my head doctor". I said smiling. "Don't make me laugh, I gotta pee". "Go pee then". "I am," she said getting up naked. I slapped her ass, and she turned around and stared. "What"? I asked her. "Yep, I'ma need some more medication. I'm having withdrawals" ...". Go pee".

"Where is the princess"? "In there watching her Disney show and eating her feast that Da king/daddy cooked". "Oh, I love the king, and I love the queen".

Chapter 11 - Da Black Top

I had done all the homework on the Clack nigga and felt that instead of me calling the nigga and warning him that I was coming, I would just show up.

(Never in life keep a schedule of your comings and goings because you may not make it to your next spot. Show up instead of announcing you're coming)

I took BQ with me and had Stix and Hasko follow me at a distance in a stuffer. When I pulled in at the baby mansion, Stix kept driving and went to the motel room we booked in a fake Hancock. Tank cussed and flipped out because he wasn't involved in what was about to happen. Mind you, he wasn't exactly moving fast enough to be active, so I promised him a Souvenir and he was okay with it. I called the nigga Clack when I pulled in his large driveway. "Hey, Clack Clack," he answered. "Wassup Clack, dis yo boy Legendary...what's the hook"? "Shit, at the house wrapping up some loose ends. "Shit, for a minute thought you spent a nigga or something". "Naw my nigga, when the wind blows I gotta keep ahold to the string". "Kites fly and rise if you let them go". "I dig it". "Where you stationed at"? "I'm live and direct in yo driveway waiting for an invitation". "Nigga, my joint so big, I can't tell when mufuckas pull up unless they knock, but yeah my nigga come up". "I got one of my lil niggas with me". "You seen him last time we were out here". "Bring dat nigga up, he good if he with you". "Ain't nobody up yonder but me and a Clydesdale". We touched the steps and Clack opened the door wearing a wife-beater and a thick piece of jewelry around his neck, "We All We Got", chain. I smiled and embrace him, "What's up Clack man? Dis my nigga Wax". "Wassup Legendary". Reaching to shake BQ's hand, "nice to meet you Waxman, I'm Clack.

   "Nice to finally meet da Clack, my guy speaks in the best regards for you, so my respect rest with you". BQ said with a smile on his face. "No doubt, come in y 'all" "Nigga, what you in this camp doing"? "I see you stepped yo dime game up huh"? "Oh, this little thing"? He said holding Tanks chain out towards us. "It's like a herringbone my nigga, house wear" ... "I'm in this joint watching the bubble". When he said that, a nice redbone, who resembled Diamond from "Playas Club' stepped from behind a curtain naked and oiled up. "Dats live right there," Wax said, looking over the chick. "She nice for the pushing and very respectful when it comes to entertaining company". He said, pointing her to Wax. She walked over and said to Wax, "what is it you wish for"? "I like to rub on the on the genie, but I don't do so unless the man of the house grants me access". "You my niggas, peoples". "You mine to my nigga, granted on that note". With that said, he walked a little and told me to come fuck with him in the kitchen. . . So, I did. "Aye, Legendary, you wanna drink my nigga"? "Yeah, what you got in this joint"? I said, rubbing my hands together. He opened a cabinet and pointed. "You pick whatever you want," he said smiling like he was that guy. I snatched a bottle of Hennessy. "Aye, when you leave, you can take that whole bottle, I got reserves as you can tell". He laughed. "Yes Sir".

"So, for what do I owe you, the pleasure of the Legendary one to be in my driveway". "I was out this way, on my mop and glow gig". "Cleaning up on the terms of paper, from my last show". "I felt I owed the Clack a holla". "Right, when you wanna put something together my nig"? "We gone be out this way for a few days my nig, and tonight I'm just trying to mingle". "Check a few spots out". "Matter fact, what's up on the night"? "You free to show me the town"? "We can do that my nig, I'm never too busy, to show my nigga round". "Plus, I know a few spots to touch"! "Give me a ring and let me know, when and where, and I'm there". I told him, "it's 6 right now... I'ma call you bout 11 and give you a chance to mingle". "Sounds like a bet to me". "Before you leave, let me show you around the camp". "We got all tomorrow for the tour my nig", plus Wax in there enjoying the ride". "No doubt, no doubt". I embraced him again, and we both walked out to see the chick playing with her pussy, while BQ watched. "Aye Clack, she bad as a mufucka my guy, but I didn't ride the mane". "Yo bad my nigga, cause she buck like a wild bull in the rodeo"! We all laughed, except her. She looked at me seductively and tasted her fingers. "Okay, hit me Clack".

When we got to the room, Stix and Hasko was relieved to see us. "Damn, what y 'all killed the niggas by y 'all selves or something"? Stix wanted to know. "Naw, we made ol boy feel comfortable with us". "Ain't that right Wax"? I said looking at BQ. Everybody looked at BQ and smiled. "Nigga, I watched a live strip show". "I guess the nigga thought I was a fuckboy and put the bitch on me for entertainment" "Bad or normal", asked Hasko.

"Mind-blowing... the type to get a regular nigga missing" "Right" ... "Anyways, he gone hit my phone round 11, and from there we in da club". When we come out, we play Halloween and we on the freeway". "I want the nigga to see me," Stix said, "so I can take his thoughts from him". "Dats cool, but don't let nobody else see you, and search yo surroundings for cameras" ... "Me and BQ gone keep our heads low, so we can't be described" ... Have my whip out its spot and towards the yellow brick road". "Yep, I hear you Dorothy". "In three clicks we gone be home". Stix said smiling. "You ain't no poet Stix"! BQ told him. "Nah, I'm the tornado dat sweep mufuckas off they feet, til they lost and find "Oz". "So, you really the Scarecrow"? BO said. "Yep, ease on down the road" . . ."Well BQ, you the dog Toto," Hasko said. "Fuck you nigga, I'm the Tinman and I keep dis 40 oiled"! "Hasko gotta be the Heartless Lion then," I said laughing. . . "You know it Nigga"!

My phone rang at 10:50pm, and it was Clack. "Wassup Clack man"? I said when I answered the phone. "You ready for the night out and about my nig"? "Am I"? "Yes sir". I stayed up plenty nights thinking bout this chapter, and a bad bitch in da cipher... "I'm leaving the room right now". "Where I'm heading"? "You know yo way around here, a little bit"? "Enough to get where y 'all at". "We at Eskimos on Price Street". "The hood spot, by Samsung phone company"? "Yeah, that's the joint". "We in this mufucka hanging like titties". "We there my nig, where y 'all parked at"? "The front or the back"? "Hood niggas stay at the back route, just in case they need a fast escape". "Dig dat" ... "See y 'all when y 'all touch down". "Gone" ... I said hanging up the phone.

When me and BQ touched the spot, we didn't see any cameras inside or outside the joint. I pressed the button on my phone, signaling Hasko and Stix that the spot was clean of footage. '1' meant cameras and '2' meant none, all without talking. "Hey, my nigga Clack, what's the weather report"? "Making it rain in this bitch"! "I see" ... "Deez my folk's right over here," he said taking me to where his two potnas sat with a crowd of females. I nodded my head and said what's up. "Yeah, my nigga, mingle, we up in this bitch". "Yep". "Wax spotted his genie from earlier and had her by his poker machine touching buttons. She whispered to Wax, "I like you". "I like to be liked, but I need the highest rank and that's a love quote". BQ said smiling. "I liked how you didn't take advantage, of the opportunity earlier and only touched me lightly" ... She purred. "I didn't wanna offend Clack". "My man's got mad respect for him". "Dats what's up". "I'm Dynasty". "Nice to meet you ma" ... "You too beautiful for show and tail, you should be stuffed and hung up with the rest of the trophies". She blushed and said, "thank you and here's my phone number". "I'm not Clacks girl, he just pays for entertainment" ... "Okay, I can go for that". "Call me sometime, and its above entertainment on the behalf of us". "Yep, will do Dynasty".

The club was jumping, and it was a lot going on. I walked around, until Clack approached me talking about going bowling. "Wassup Clack"? I asked him, as he walked up. "Let's go to the bowling alley my nigga, have some fun". "You bowl"? "Do I"? "My nigga, I'm a knock down artist when it comes to pins in the way of my bowl game". "I'ma send these hoes in front of us to get some lanes" ... "A hundred a game too much"? "Dey ain't stop making money, when Clack got some". "Say a rack a game"! "Bet... my money long my nigga". "Not easy to knock me down". "I'ma show you better than I can tell you, so speak to me I after pluck the turkey my nigga... at least three strikes back to back". "Nuff said" . . . "I'ma grab this nigga Wax and let him know we on our way out. I'll meet y 'all out back". "Okay my nig".

I touched BQ and told him it was show time. I got outside and pressed three buttons and made it to the back of the joint. I seen two niggas walking our way, they passed us and lingered for a minute. When me and BQ make it to the car by the alley, he reaches in the trunk and comes out with a coat and a mask. "Legend, I'm with dis ride my nig, I put that on Stink". "Okay, hurry up". I told him. BQ walked up to Stix, and Hasko and nodded.

When Clack and his potnas hit the corner, it was four niggas, no females. Stix stepped out with his mask raised, "aye lil man", he said pointing the 40 cal. with the thirty-round clip hanging like blue balls. "Long time, no see, my nigga...member me"? Before they could react, the sparks started to fly. Bam! BQ shot the new booty in the head. The two niggas with Clack separated and started to run. That's when Hasko' s thunder came alive, hitting the big nigga in the back. Which spun him around, to where his chest came apart from the rapid slugs. The other nigga, BQ chased, ran right into me. I jumped out my whip and asked him, "what's up"? "Some niggas started shooting" ... "Clack over there"! "Where"? I asked, looking in the direction he came from. He turned to show me, and I pulled my 40 out and made his brain a peep-hole. Stix had Clack on the ground, after shooting him five times in the shoulders and legs. People was screaming and running everywhere. "Next time you rob and shoot a nigga, make sure you finish the job"! Stix said, snatching Tanks' necklace. "Dis for my nigga and me"! Stix shot Clack so many times, in the head that his neck was severed from the body. He also snatched his phone, then ran. . .

When we was on the freeway, I cracked the bottle Clack had given me and yelled, "to the nigga Clack's Departure". On the way home, we stopped and tossed all the guns in the lake and burned the mask. We slid by on Tank, who wanted to hear the details. I spared him, and just went in my pocket and tossed him his chain. "Ain't shit to talk about my nigga". "We all going to church this week, and I expect you there for repentance and a new way to look at life". "Damn Legend, don't let me find out, in yo past life you was a Deacon or something". "They say Jesus is the doctor, and he came here to heal those who's not well" ... "I'm sick nigga and need what he has to offer". "Amen". Hasko said. Tank shook my hand and embraced me, as well as the others... then we left.

(Repentance Day)

Since Yasmine had been back, from the track she had changed her whole lifestyle and become a member of Allen Temple Church, on 8th and Skidmore. Her relationship with Shontay was better than before she left. Her, Sissy, Shontay and Tanisha was always together. Yasmine invited us to the church, so we all made the guest appearance at Allen Temple.

(And I mean everybody came!)

Me, Shontay, Eni'yah, Sissy, both Jamie's, Tank, Tanisha, and they kids, Raw, Sasha and they son, BJ, Anjanique and they son B2, Rodney, Megan, Jamie's mom La'Nette and Shawny

Stix lil sis.

We packed in to hear the word of God and listen to Pastor Menefee. He spoke of the lost sheep of the Shepherd and the wolves who scattered the herd. "God don't like the big bad wolf, who blows smoke and ignorance in his field of sheep. In fact, he dislikes lies so much that although he ended such world in the flood. In the days of Noah, he promised us a safety net from that happening again. That safety nets name is Jesus Christ, his own son, who was sacrificed, that we may live another life outside of sin.

We don't have to bathe in the mud and dirt. We can bathe in the blood of Jesus, our Savior,

Da Black Top (second half)

"SOMEBODY SAY AMEN"!

(AMEN)

"SOMEBODY SAY PRAISE GOD"

(PRAISE GOD)

"IT'S BEEN PEOPLE IN THIS BOOK WHO WASTED TIME WORSE THAN ANY OF US IN THIS CONGREGATION", PAUL WAS A MURDERER, SAMSON SLEPT WITH A PROSTITUTE, MOSES WAS A KILLA, DAVID A MAN IN THE ACT OF ADULTERY, JONAH RAN FROM THE WORD OF GOD, PETER DENIED THE VERY CHRIST IN WHOM HE HAD SEEN PERFORM MIRACLES, ALL IN THE ACT OF REPENTANCE WERE SAVED!

"CAN I HEAR A HALLELUJAH"

(HALLELUJUAH)

"PRAISE GOD IF THEY CAN BE FORGIVEN FOR THEM TYPE OF DEEDS, KNOW THOSE OF US HERE HAVE A CHANCE. DECEIVE YO SHEPHARD NOT AND LISTEN TO THE CALLING OF HIS VOICE COME HOME MY CHILD . . . YES LORD. JOHN 8:4-11"

"IT WAS A WOMAN WHO WAS CAUGHT IN THE VERY ACT OF ADULTERY AND WAS BROUGHT TO JESUS" ...

"TEACHER, TEACHER, WE CAUGHT THIS WOMAN IN THE ACT OF HAVING SEX AND BY THE COMMANDMENTS OF MOSES IT SAYS WE SHOULD STONE HER" ...

"WHAT DO YOU SAY GOOD TEACHER"? JESUS, KNOWING THE HEARTS OF WHO BROUGHT THIS WOMAN IN FRONT OF HIM KNEW THE TRICK IN WHICH SATAN WAS TRYING TO PLAY. HE KNELT AND WROTE SOMETHING IN THE DIRT WITH HIS FINGER, WHEN HE STOOD BACK UP HE REPLIED, "HE WHO'S WITHOUT SIN CAST THE FIRST STONE"

"THEN HE BENT BACK DOWN AND FINISHED WRITING IN THE DIRT. WHEN JESUS LOOKED UP, THERE WAS NOBODY THERE BUT THE WOMAN, BEING THAT SHE WASN'T DEAD MUST HAVE MEANT THAT ALL THOSE WHO ACCUSED HER OF HER WRONG HAD WRONGS IN WHICH THEY WERE FORGIVEN FOR, OR SHE WOULD HAVE BEEN DEAD ALREADY SO HE ASK HER HIMSELF, "WOMAN, IS THERE NO ONE LEFT TO PERSECUTE YOU"

"THE WOMAN ANSWERED, "NO TEACHER" AND HE SAID, THEN GO AND SIN NO MORE". HE SAID IF THE LORD, WHO IS GODS ONLY BEGOTTEN SON, CAN'T THROW A STONE AT SOMEBODY HE KNOW HAD FAULT, NEITHER WILL I PLACE JUDGMENT ON NO MAN, WOMAN OR CHILD FOR LEADING A LIFE OF SIN, BECAUSE I MYSELF HAVE SINNED ALIKE. IF ANYBODY TODAY IS IN THE LORD'S HOUSE WHO CAN POINT A FINGER AT THE PERSON NEXT TO YOU OR TURN YO NOSE UP TOWARDS ANY IN THIS HOUSE OF AMENDS, THEN YOU'RE IN THE WRONG HOUSE AND MAYBE YOU'RE NOT SEEKING THE WORD OF GOD BECAUSE JESUS FORGAVE, FOR US TO BELIEVE AND SEEK BETTER IN LIFE".

"SPEAK THE TRUTH, RATHER YOU LIKE ME AFTER THIS SERMON OR NOT, KNOW AS A MAN OF GOD KEEP IT REAL. IF YOU FEEL LIKE YOU'RE BETTER THAN THE NEXT PERSON, IT'S NOT A GODLY GESTURE, IT'S THOSE OF THE DEVIL, BEING HE WANTED TO BE ABOVE GOD. IF YOU AINT NEVER STRUGGLED IN LIFE AND FELT LOST THEN YOU HAVE NO NEED FOR THE LORD

ME, PERSONALLY, I'M LOOKING FOR JESUS EVERY DAY AND I'MA REMAIN SUCH TIL HE COMES TO TAKE ME WITH HIM"

(everybody clapped)

"RAISE YO HANDS IF YOU NEED JESUS"

(Even the kids raised they hands)

"WELL, WE DONE START YO JOURNEY TODAY BY ASKING THE LORD JESUS INTO YOUR LIVES... BOW YO HEADS"

"FATHER, I COME TO YOU TODAY AS A LOST SOUL IN SEARCH OF MY LORD AND SAVOR. KNOW THAT IN ORDER TO RECEIVE HIS GRACE OF FORGIVENESS MUST FIRST BELIEVE HE DIED FOR MY SINS. SECONDLY, I HAVE TO ADMIT TO MY WRONGS AND ASK TO BE FORGIVEN. LORD, FORGIVE ME OF MY SINS I AM A SINNER, THEN YOU AND I HAVE TO FORGIVE THOSE"

"WHO HAVE WRONGED US, AND NOT CAST A STONE,

FOR THEY AND YOU ARE OF THE SAME NATURE, A
SINNER ASK THE LORD FOR STRENGTH NOT TO BE
JUDGMENTAL TOWARDS OTHERS AND TO CARRY THE
BURDENS YOU HAD, I SAID THE BURDENS YOU HAD
BEFORE YOU FOUND HIM, JESUS IN THE LORD'S NAME
CAST OUT HATRED, DECEIT, ENVY AND DEMONS AND
ADD AN ABUNDANCE OF LOVE, HONOR, HONESTY AND
RESPECT, IN THE NAME OF JESUS CHRIST OF
NAZARETH I PRAY. THE HOLY SPIRIT TAKE HOLD OF
YOU AND YOU LEAVE HERE LOST TO THE WORLD BUT
FOUND IN JESUS CHRIST AMEN"

(AMEN)

When the offering tray came around, I believe I had
$2,800 in cash on me and I threw all of it in there and watched
as all of those who came with me did the same.

(Emptied pockets for the Lord's house)

In all, we probably put in over $15,000. The word preached
was at its best and we all felt the grace of forgiveness.

Before we left, we rushed off to speak to the pastor and thanked him for such a powerful message. "Hey, how you doing Pastor Menefee"? I asked approaching him. "How are you doing young man"? "I see you new to the church, but I hope you come back and visit us again". "I'm doing great now, that I felt what the message meant". "I wouldn't mind coming back, to hear God at his finest" ... "The way you preached the word, God is smiling". I said smiling. "Amen, young brotha". "My name is La 'Real Sykes, and all the people in those last four rows are my family" ... "Just wanted to say you did a great job, speaking the word of God".

"Thank you La 'Real, you and yo family is welcome anytime"! "Thank you," said shaking his hand, "Do you do weddings"? "If so, what's the price"? "I may owe you more than I'm able to pay son, let's start with you and yo family having dinner at my house tonight". "Um... that's fine. I will only be bringing my fiancé and our daughter Eniyah".

"No problem, here's my number". "Does seven sound like an ok time"? "Sounds great Pastor Menefee". "We are eating a feast, so come hungry"! "Okay, see you at seven". "You Believe in Magic"? Before we all got in our cars and departed, Yasmine thanked us for coming and welcomed us back anytime. She rubbed Shontay's stomach and smiled at me.

"Bro, you turned out to be a better man than most and thank you for loving my sister enough to help get us back on track". Shontay looked at me, and I shrugged my shoulders. "It's no problem sis," I said, hugging Yasmine. "I'm glad you came back home to use all"! She smiled and winked at me.

(OKAY, ALLOW ME TO TELL THE WHOLE TRUTH TO YALL, SINCE IT'S IN YO MIND) ...

When Shontay was getting close to graduating from College, I noticed a look on her face and asked her what was wrong? She told me nothing and gave me a fake smile. So, when she got up from the couch, she accidentally left a picture of her and Yasmine on the end table. When I seen that, I went to see my uncle Magnify in the Sheridan Federal Prison. I asked him to get me Pretty Tony's number and he did. (Pimps respect pimps)

I called Tony, and told him that I was Magnify's nephew, and Yasmine's brother-in-law. He told me my uncle had told him that I was gonna call. What can the pimpin, do for a gangsta? I asked him how much it would cost, for the release of Yasmine's contract and for him to not ever say a word to her again? First, he laughed, then said, "you for real"? "I'm serious as a gorilla, out da cage"! "Young blood, give me 30 stacks and I don't know, Yasmine or you on the pimpin". "I'ma give you 35... make sure my sister-in-law on the plane tonight; and that you keep to yo word, because about my banana I'll go apes. You got a bank account where I can send it to"? He gave me the routing number, and all went peaches and herb.

(Now, why didn't I tell Shontay that it was me who did it and blamed it on Sissy? Because details is not what describes who legend is, my faithfulness and heart is. So, I blamed sissy and told her to get the apartment and everything ready for when Yasmine came home).

I told everybody that the pastor invited me to his house. They gave me the thumbs-up and told me to call when I left from over there, to make sure we got home safe. At 6:30pm, I called the pastor and he asked was I on my way. I told him already in close route and I would be pulling up in a few minutes. He obliged and let the line drop.

"Baby, so he just invited us here like that"? Shontay asked me after I hung up. "Yep, but he seemed a little shocked when I told him my name... it was strange"! "I bet, the preacher asking you over as if he been knowing us forever". "I guess when you in the life of God, you do things out the blue". "Yeah, ol preach" ... "Eni'yah"? "Huh mommy"? "Make sure you be on yo best behavior, okay"? "Okay mommy, I will". "We here," I said to my family. We got out and walked to the door and knocked. "Hey La 'Real, glad you and your family could come". The pastor said, opening the door.

"Thank you for inviting us Pastor". "This is my fiancé Shontay and our beautiful daughter Eni'Yah". "Hi", they both said to the pastor. "Glad to meet you beautiful ladies". His wife came and greeted us all. "This is my beautiful wife Candice", the pastor said introducing her. "How are you doing ma'am"? "I'm La 'Real and this is my queen-to-be, Shontay and our princess Eni'yah". "What a pleasure to meet you lovely people," she said. "Um... can I take the ladies with me and give the men a few minutes"? I smiled, "of course you can". When they walked out the room, the pastor escorted me to have a seat. "Um, La 'Real. . . I would like you to know, I would love to do yo wedding". "If after we have this conversation you still want me to". I smiled and nodded. "It's something else we need to discuss, if you're willing to do so".

"After that sermon you preached today, I'm willing to hear whatever it is you have to say"! "In 1978, I met a beautiful woman named Marie Sykes at a house party of some mutual friends. We danced and drank and partied," my face changed, "and we began to see one another". "I was addicted to cocaine and made the choice to have unprotected sex with Marie". "Without" he raised his finger "being stable as a man or in a financial way".

"So" ... I started to say. "Please allow me to finish," he cut me off, and I nodded". "I involved myself into heavy drugs and crimes and went to jail for killing a man in the robbery of his home". "I was sentenced to serve sixteen years". "When I found out I had a son by yo mom, she was no longer here, and you were fifteen somewhere". "I tried to contact yo grandmother, but I was told that she lived in a state to where her comprehension had left her". "Stacy had been killed and yo uncle Steven was in the Feds in Atlanta" ...

"When you walked in the church today and we met face to face, I looked into yo mom's eyes but saw my own reflection". "I am the father that you never had the chance to meet" ..." I'm La 'Real Menefee, and you are my son La 'Real"! I couldn't breathe, and my eyes blurred up" ..." what he just say"? I thought to myself. I spoke up, "um, nice to finally meet you". On them conditions, of me being who you said I was to you" (a son, the words wouldn't come out) "don't mean I won't pay for my own wedding and you don't owe me nothing". He fidelity moved... I couldn't be mad at a man, that I never met and didn't know what his circumstances was. I vowed to be better than him, for my kids and wife. "I forgive you La 'Real and we can make it work, after the storm". "If God see fit to do so". I said. "Amen, La 'Real, now we got that out the way, can we eat"? He asked, holding his hand out for me to take. It started as a shake but ended with him embracing me.

We ate a feast . . . 24 years had passed, but I was returned to the prodigal father; I had grown up referring to as the Magician. The man that I never knew existed. A preacher's son... who would have thought? God will find you, no matter what it is you're into.

After leaving my father's house, when we were on the ride home and our daughter was asleep. I decided to open up to Shontay, "Baby"? I said to her. "Huh"? She said looking at me. "Did you enjoy yo self and the meal at the pastor's house"? "Yes, I did, but he kept looking at Eni'yah and smiling". "I seen him too". "What do you think he was thinking"? "Probably to have a granddaughter is so precious"!

"Yeah, she is something, huh"? "Everything," I said kissing Shontay's hand. "Um, I made arrangements for the pastor to do our wedding, if that's okay with you"? "What"? "That's if you will still have me, and you ready to change yo last name", I said smiling. "When"? "In the next month or two before your stomach gets too big". "Stop playing baby"! "I'm not," I said with that look, to where she knew I was being real. "Yes, I'm ready baby"! "It's December next month and Christmas next month but a perfect time... Christmas sound good to you"? I asked her. "Yes baby, that's perfect. I gotta gather my team together and we can pull this off". She said kissing me and then asked, "you ready"? "Like yesterday, I would have married you after the puzzle we completed, but we were too young"! "You are too crazy". "Oh yeah, the pastor name is La 'Real too". "How you know all that"? "Because he told me, and he also told me why my name and his was the same"! Shontay looked at me, "Yep, after all this time I finally met the man that made me"! "He's yo dad"? "Yes ma'am". "That's why he kept looking at Eni'yah like that, because she is his granddaughter". "Bingo"

The females had been too busy getting all the gifts, invitations, flowers, and everything else together to show us any attention. Me and the fellas went and got sized up. I picked Hasko to be the best man. We decided the wedding colors would be of a king's nature; purple and white. We went with all white suits with purple hankies, ties, vest, and white and purple Jordan's. It was double hectic like, but when it was time we shined! My daughter and nephew lil Jamie was the flower girl and the ring bearer. We had to do this in a big space and invited a lot of people. Before I forget, Tanks son was with my nephew and his daughter was with my daughter as ring bearers and flower girls.

Everybody was there from BQ, BJ, Raw and Hasko to Angie, Anjanique, Sasha, Yasmine, Kristie, and Jamie's two sisters, Shawny and Jasmine. The wedding song was that Monica, "For You I Will". When that song came on, you could hear the crowd say, "I love this song". I stood in the front looking on, as mine and Tanks daughters threw flowers everywhere in the church. I turned to look at Tank and Stix and smiled. Shontay came out escorted by her dad Rodney. Sissy was escorted by BQ, and Tanisha by Raw. It was the best day of all our lives, because we became united with the women who made us feel complete in front of God and our families. (Merry Christmas!)

BQ ended up using the phone number Dynasty gave him, and she answered... Mind you, this is six months after the weddings and 7 months since the Clack incident. They met in Longview, close to Tacoma, Washington. "Hey Wax," she said, "what took you so long to call me"? "I've been on tour with my record label". "I was like, damn, I kept it 1 milli wit dude... what, he don't want all this", she said pointing at her body. "I prefer the woman see within, then just to settle for the fast route". "You crazy Wax, but sexy at the same time... "Where can we go right now"? "I got a room at the Hilton if that's what you mean by, "where can we go right now?"" "I thought you'd never ask"!

Until this day Dynasty, nor anybody else, knew Wax real identity, but this nigga fucked around and got a room in his real name. Not only was he not to do what he did, but he was never to meet with a female he met at a dead man's house. Clack had played the right nigga as the fuckboy, because the appearance of Dynasty had BQ's mind missing. When they went in the room, she stripped. "I don't have no master now, so the genie is free to grant all yo wishes". "Lay down and allow me to scan yo body". "As you wish daddy". As soon as she complied, he began touching her in the sensitive spots. "Wax, taste me, everything is well sugared and sweet". He sucked on the breast, he hadn't seen since that day at Clack's. "I loved yo body, from the first glance".

knew you wanted this pussy..., take what you want". "Oh, and I like it in all the holes," she said smiling. BQ reached for a condom but she caught his hand, "you can turn on all the lights and inspect my pussy closely, ain't nothing wrong with my shit". "You fuck me, you fuck me all natural"! "Dats how you want it"? "Yes daddy, all of you"! "Nothing to hold back any feeling".

BQ slid his dick in her windpipes, and let her tonsils blow the flute. "Ohh, take it all" he said, toes giving out. She sucked his dick and massaged his balls. "Damn, I'm in love Dynasty". She stopped and told him, "Lay back daddy". He did, and she climbed up on top of him, and rode him until the race was almost over. "No daddy don't cum yet! I want it in every way first"! She rolled over and lay on her back and slipped his dick in missionary. "Yes daddy, fuck this pussy. This is what you wanted? To be deep inside me, huh"? "Yes, I wanted it," he said lifting her legs, "this is what I wanted"! "Shit daddy...right there... right there" ... "You like this dick, huh"? "No, I love this dick fuck me harder" ... "I'ma beat the lining out this joint". "Aww daddy, I'm cummin...stick it in my ass now". He pulled it out her pussy and stuck it in her ass as she demanded. "Oh daddy, beat it up"! "Beat that ass up"! He was pumping hard and seen the cum squirt on his stomach, "Harder"! He raised her legs past her head and beat the asshole like a plunger in a toilet. She showered the whole bed and began to shake uncontrollably. "Fuck me from the back"! When he did, she lifted her ass and dropped her head in the pillow and began to fuck him back hard.

"I'm finna Cum"! BQ Said. "Don't stop daddy, I want it inside me! All of it"! He came in her pussy full throttle, "Ahh shit"! "Yes, cum for me daddy"! He did...within minutes of cummin she got up and for the first time he noticed the tattoo, "Property of Clack" under her left ass cheek. "You like that pussy, huh daddy"? She asked him. "I love dat shit". "Come and lay down and take a nap with me". "Okay". She said and laid down. BQ dozed off, when he woke up he looked to the left, where Dynasty had been when he went to sleep. Instead of her he saw and heard the police scream, "Freeze motherfucker, police"! With their guns drawn. His first thought was what he had done, to have the police in his room until he looked over and saw Dynasty's face clothes. "He raped me"! She said crying and pointing at BQ.

Tank got the call, at 6am the next morning. "Hello". he answered. "U. S West has a collect call from BQ, at a Kent county jail," "Kent"? Tank said to himself confused."... If you accept press one" ... Tank pressed '1', and said "Hello"? "Man, what's up bro"?

"Nigga, why you in Washington"? "Man bro, bad acting"! "Chick or Stick"? "Chick, man they charged me with snatchin the panties"! Tank laughed, "Yeah right"! "On Stink my nig, the "We All We Got", bitch". "Who is that"? "They say, yo chain hang low, da return souvenir". "No, don't tell me the dog chased the cat and went for the meet and greet, pushed and poked . . . and freeze mufucka"? "Yeah exactly, den lost my mind, felt R-Kelly fast bump and grind, wouldn't hurt the Waxman but it turned out to be owned by lost Souls of the back Cracker, and made moves to seal the past tense for a lil nigga" ... "Damn, Angie gone gymnastic"! "I know, damn" ... "Did the kid go naked like first thing in the morning on drain"? "Or was there candy wrapped, covered no peanuts"? "Regular unleaded, all gas no break. ...even the trunk was opened and no luggage". "Fuck, what the bail look like"? "None, for the fact Roman candle, ready for the 4th of July". "New, right"? "Pine sol, Mr. Clean". "Okay I'ma push the button every time you call bro... let me round this lawyer up so he can come spring you". "Ray Dupree will be there within a few hours". "I love you bro, don't let them be too mad at me when you tell them... I fucked up". "Ok, one milli. "Hit me back after the attorney has left". "Yep". "Gone".

Tank hit my phone at about 7, "Legend"? "What's up Tank"? I said in a sleepy voice and getting out the bed, so my wife wouldn't wake up. "You still in bed, with sis"?

"No, what's up"? "BQ in the county jail in Washington on rape charges"! "What"? "Yeah, the Dynasty bitch from out there, with the midgets"! "Hell nah bro... you're lying, right"? "Nah, we at one milli my nigga". "How he see that bitch way out there"? "He figured he could tap and leave... no biggie but ol girl set him up". "Let him do everything to her under the sun and he woke up to the police". "Naw my nig... protected or bareback". "Naked; nut everywhere and a firecracker". "New or used"? "Mr. Clean, Pine Sol". "Fuck dat shit, dat nigga outta pocket". "Dat was over after the head-and-shoulders . . . and he went back"? "Calm down bro". Shontay appeared, stomach getting big, "What's wrong baby"? she asked me.

"Nothing is wrong mommy, I'll be back in the bed in a minute". She looked, but I disappeared in seconds. "I sent the lawyer down there already". "Ray Dupree"? "Yep". "What's his bail look like"? "Nada, they say he used the pistol in the crime" . . .

"Nigga, this shit is mind-blowing! "When I see lil bro I'ma cuss his as out". "Da game was over, life goes on" ... "I know

116

but don't be too hard on the young cock hound". "We need to find the chick and throw a few stacks at her, so she can at least free him from the rape . . . on the stick though, he gone have to stand up for that". "Yeah, I'm gonna get back in this bed, before my bill collector come out here again". "I will put something together on that tip ASAP". "Okay, hit me when you rise and shine my nig". "Gone".

     I went back to lay down with my wife and rub her tummy" . . .Why you so nervous babe"? she wanted to know. "What makes you think I'm nervous"? "I can feel you when you're not around, so you don't think I can feel you when you here in my face"? "It's ok mommy, I promise". "Hopefully you just did that, to protect something or someone you love, because you've never intentionally lied to me before"! She moved my hand off her stomach. "Baby, I love you". I said putting my hand back on her stomach. "I would never lie to harm you or my household, but its things from the street that I don't need to involve you in". "Ok," she said, rubbing her hand over mine. "Cuss BQ out for me too, since he's the reason for my husband being out the bed this early". I rocked her back to sleep, without another word.

Chapter 12 - Blood-N-Blood Out

When I woke up, I had a meal in front of me, and Shontay had dropped of Eni'yah at the daycare. She called herself, looking for me to explain this morning. She was just sitting there staring at me. "Why are you sitting there, staring at me like that Shontay"? "Because for some reason, my stomach had a bad feeling this morning". "When you didn't wanna talk about, what Tank was telling you in front of me".

"After you knew I was woke... who is she La 'Real"? In my most calm voice, I said "Shontay there never will be a woman that comes between us". "I'm yo husband, and when I wasn't can't no female, ever begin to describe the feeling of my dick". "I married you for eternity and gave you all of me because I'm in love with what I have in you". "Can't no other woman be Shontay". "When I didn't tell you what was going on, it was for yo own good". "If the police ever show up, at the door-step; telling you yo husband is a murderer, you didn't know any of that". "I am yo husband, so I may owe some type of rap on the ordeal. BQ is in trouble, and the type of trouble he's in, could lead to missing husbands from their families for a lifetime". And yes, I'm one".

"Oh my God," she said with fear in her eyes. "See, that's why I leave a lot unsaid, but beyond that bullshit, come here and look me in my eyes". She came over, "Please never in the rest of our lives put, another's pussy nor make in our relationship". "I am of a rare breed, and if my dick caused me to sin rather live with it, cut it off". "You are my queen, and I don't need nothing but the family that you have blessed me with". "Do you understand"? "Yes, I do". "Now, don't stress our baby inside yo stomach, by trying to figure out what's going on". "Allow me to connect these dots, to make the wrong right"! "K". "Plus, we already went to God's house for repentance". I said. "Allen Temple". I raised my eyes and kissed her.

I called Stix and asked where Sissy was at. "She right here, why"? What's up bro"? "Open the door, bodyguard". "Ok, Darkwing duck". I walked in the house and was greeted by my nephew wearing a championship belt, as soon as I passed Stix. "What's up boy"? I said tackling my nephew. "No uncle, you cheated"! "How"? "You gotta say go"! "Well, I seen you with the belt on like you were the champ and I felt like I wanted to pin you, so I could be the champ". "My daddy didn't count me out, huh daddy"? "Nope". Stix said smiling. "Go," I said...and what do you know; they all jumped me, even Sissy one, two, three. "I'm still the champ uncle"! "Yeah, you are boy". "Next time, I'ma bring my team for all of y 'all"! "We still gone win"! "Never, we want the title too bad and we will get it by all means"! "Never" . . . "Aye boy, let me talk to yo dad and mom for a minute but when I'm done ...ewww." "Okay". "Wassup bro"? Sissy asked me. "Can we sit for this"? I asked.

"Yeah, my nigga, what's up"? Stix said. "We need you and Sissy to take a trip to. Eugene and find a female named Dynasty for us"! "To Eugene"? Stix said confused. "Clack reasons bro, and the past maybe wrecking futures". His eyes got real big-like. "How? With no snaps or nobody"? "BQ is in jail in Washington, for meeting up with Dynasty, on false rape charges and a gun" . . . "What that got to do with y 'all"? Sissy asked. Stix breathed, then grabbed her hands. "It has everything to do with us babe, because we ended the lives of those responsible for me and Tanks shooting". She hit me in the back of the head. "Bro y 'all was supposed to be at a damn show, not killing people! Dats why you were smiling, that day I came in after his first show Jamie". We both put our heads down, "Fresh out the hospital, huh? ... Do you know what I went through when I thought you were gonna die Jamie"? "Babe". "Don't you dare babe me right now nigga"! She said hitting him upside the head. "La 'Real, I'm very disappointed in you". Not just because of him but you're the only family I had before I made a family with him" ... "Be truthful with me, on mama, about everything and please be so kind as to not leave one thing out"!

"The niggas who did that to Tank and Stix wanted to rap with me, so I rocked him to sleep as if we were cool". "How did you know who he was, if he had a mask on when he shot them"? "When I was talking to Stix on the phone after the show, the dude approached me, and Stix heard the voice of the man who shot him in the background". "He described him from here and was very accurate". "So, you killed him"? "No, I kicked it with him, and then we killed him". Stix said. "How, if you were here with me"? "Not that night, bout a week later". "Then we came back and went to church to repent". I cut in. "I knew something was fishy about all of us at church" ...

"Ok, about BQ now"? "The dude who got it, had a female at his house who tried to seduce BQ, but we were on the mission". "So, she gave him the number and he called months later". "He called the chick from where the dude got killed? After"? "Yep and took her to a room in Washington trying to be slick". "So, she gave him the pussy and then called rape"? "Yep," "So what you want me to do"? "Kill the bitch"? "No, I want you to find the girl and have her write an affidavit that she lied". "Get it notarized and give her this money to keep her mouth closed and forget BQ exist" ... "Which she thinks his name is Wax". "More like Wax dat ass...what if she refuses"? "She won't" . . . "Both of y 'all make me sick, when do leave"?

"Today, in like an hour". "I got the briefcase in my trunk". "How much"? "Start at ten and go as far as 40,000 if need be". "Jamie going with me, so you taking my baby with you". "Okay". "When Angie find out about this, she gonna" Stix interrupted, "she not gone find out'. "This is like the Gerald ordeal"! "When he gets out, he got some explaining to do, but we can't jeopardize everybody's freedom". "How, if it was only one person died"? "You mean four; everybody with us is in jeopardy"! I said. "Four went in and four died". Stix finished. "Okay". Sissy said getting the picture.

They left and went on the move. In the meantime, the lawyer made it out there to see BQ and told him the gig. As far as, in a few hours the rape charge would be dropped but the gun would remain. He understood that and asked when could he expect bail and was told between 24-72 hours from now. In the meantime, Sissy and Stix arrived and got a room. It was too late for them to get anything signed, the bank was closed so, they went out separately. Stix went to meet females in the hood spots, in which he felt would know Dynasty. Sissy went to meet the grinders and the cats, who held a lil change, who may know the Dynasty chick. Of Course, Sissy made a bigger impact because she had the hips and ass, to move a married man. She called Stix, "Hello"? he answered. "Babe, I'm on". She told him. "Yep, where you at"? "On my way back to the room". "In route now, like four minutes". "Gone". Sissy said hanging up. Stix looked at his phone and smile, 'gone' he said to himself.

When Stix walked in the room, he was greeted by Dynasty dancing for his wife. "There you are Keith, I thought maybe you had got lost, Happy Birthday"! "Aww babe, you didn't have to go find company, you have always been enough for me"! "I brought you the best in the escort business... what's yo name again baby girl"? "Dynasty". She said looking at Stix. "Dats what's up, I see you're worth it". "How much this run us babe"? "$500 for two hours". "What do yo services consist of"? "Both of y 'all can fuck me, anything that consist of two hours, the rest is up to y 'all"! "Well, I'm trying to promote yo career; and allow you to earn a lot of money, but being that

I'm tired it will have to wait til tomorrow, if that's possible"? "How is that, if she paid me 500 already tonight"? "I need to see you tomorrow in the morning around 9am". "Dat cost"! "That's not a problem, we are not gonna need yo services tonight". "I'ma give my wife the birthday dick before I share, but I do want some tomorrow morning". "I'ma allow you to keep the 500 she already gave you, give you 500 more in the morning". "Do you think you can do that"? "I mean, a thousand free dollaz"?

"Shit, I'm cool with that"! "Put yo clothes back on and let me tend to my pussy, Ms. Dynasty". "Okay Keith and Sonia, 9am right"? "9am and I got more doe, from where that came from for you". "I'm here" ... she said walking out of the room...a thousand dollars richer.

"What, you didn't want to look and play around first"? "Sha'Day, you can be upset about what I did, but please don't offend me on them terms"! "I don't play jack and the box my dick is for who married and my heart for my household...so outside of that, what do I need"? "Any other man would have wanted that pass". "I can name two, who would die before they stuck something that wasn't who they love, and I'm one of the two". "What BQ do ain't got shit to do with Stix". "I'm a man and I'm very much in control of me, plus look what happen to him playing Russian Roulette with his dick"? "He almost got all of us cracked"! "Either you trying to earn brownie points, or you getting smarter". "Let's go to our room so you can give me some of that juice". "Who said you're getting some"?

"Them hard things pointing at me through yo shirt, and the way you keep lickin yo lips"! "Okay, maybe just a sample". She said heading to the other room across the hall.

When Stix woke Sissy up it was 7:15am. "Babe"? he said. "Huh"? "Oh, now I can call you babe again"? "Naw I'm playing, did you bring the printer in"? "I wrote the letter on the laptop sweetie". "Oh okay, I'll hook it up in the other room". "Okay, and what you mean about 'oh, you can call me babe again"? "Don't ever not call me that'. "I don't care how mad I am, just be scared of losing you is all". "You my queen, and the only time you will ever lose me is when we both pass away of old age and even then I'ma follow you and open the doors for you". "I love you"! "Ditto". They ate and made love again.

At 9am they heard a tap on the door. "Who is it"? Sissy called out. "Dynasty". The voice said on the other side of the door. Sissy opened the door in a t-shirt and booty shorts. "Hey, see yo word is good as gold, huh"? "Y 'all good peoples and I'ma always be a woman, of my word above all"! "I see". Sissy said, licking her lips. "Hey Keith, Happy Birthday"! Dynasty said, dropping her coat to the ground and standing asshole naked. "Hey, before we get down and dirty with the hanky panky gig, I got a gift for you but there's something you have to do for me". "What is that"? "Anything for y 'all"! Stix opened the briefcase that Legend gave him, but with only 10 thousand in it and not the other 30. He wanted her to see it. "Damn, that looks like a lot of money". "What y 'all want me to do, have y 'all baby or something"? "Naw, we already have five kids, come over here and read this letter". "All I need you to is sign it in front of a notary, at the bank".

She read it, "Oh, y 'all Wax peoples"? "He's my artist and I need him to fulfill the contract he signed with my label". "So, you ain't gonna kill me, or nothing"? "Why would I do that"? "Do it look like we those type of people"? "Plus, you said me and my wife good peoples". "I'll do it, but I thought he had something to do with a few murders down here"! "I don't know nothin bout no murders, and I don't think he do either if he allowed you to trick him so easily with the pussy". "Do you think he that smart"? "Yeah, you right Keith". "I'm sorry". "I'ma send my wife with you and when you get back here, I'ma give you this 10 thousand cash, deal"? "Ok". "Put yo clothes on, and never take them off for another man unless he deserves to see what you have under them". "Real women respect themselves".

"I hear you, and I appreciate what yo guys are doing for me". They left and came back with all that was promised. "Nice doing business with you Dynasty". Stix told her handing her the money. "No problem," she said and left. "Babe, did you go in the bank with her"? "I'm in the game, not just around it"! "I heard that...Lady Stix, huh"?

"You betta know it"! When Sissy and Stix made it back to the town, they had already faxed the affidavit to the lawyer. "Glad to see y 'all made up". I said. "Shut up boy. "Where Shontay and my babies at"? "The store, getting something to eat for us". "Y 'all hungry, right"? "Hell yeah, my nig". Stix said. "What the paper go for"? I asked them. "10, I mean 11 racks". He told me back. "Put the rest in my nephew's bank account". "That's after I take a few thousand, to take me and the females shopping. Shit, if only they knew what our loving husbands were capable of". She said looking at me and Stix. "You got that one Sissy, and thanks for saving our asses"! "I am my family's keepah". "Even though they be on some wild shit, I love all of them"!

Two months after BQ's release on bail, he would plead

out to a felon in possession of a firearm and be given four years in the penitentiary. We threw bro a going away party and let him know that, money-wise, he was cool but to keep his mouth closed. He and Angie fell out over her finding out he had sexual escapades with other females. She never found out about the false rape charges. Raw and Sasha, along with they son, moved out of Portland, to North Carolina to start over fresh. He invested money into a few businesses which is doing well. BJ and Anjanique, with Lil BJ, move to Columbus. Georgia to get away from the town of gossip (Portland, Oregon). They call every day as if they still lived there.

Chapter 13 - Having Our Babies

I was laying next to Shontay in the bed when she looked at me like she was in pain, "What's wrong baby"? I asked her concerned. "My stomach hurts really bad". "Like what"? I asked, and before the words were out of my mouth I felt the bed get soaked. "Baby, my water just broke"! I looked, and it was as if she peed on me and herself. "Ok, be calm and let's get the bag we made for you". "Okay, I'm calm. Where Eni'yah at"? "In the living room," I said, getting out of the bed to gather the bag of things she had packed. "I'm glad you're here with me baby. I'm not paranoid like I was the first time"!

"Come on babe, let me help you out the house". "We gotta hurry up and get to the truck safely". "You okay"? "Are you glad you're here this time"? She said in an evil voice. "Yes babe, I'm very happy to be here with you". I said smiling. "You better had said that La 'Real, because all this pushin I'm finna do is finsta really hurt"! "I'm gonna be here all the way". "Come on Eni'yah, mommy is having the baby"! "Yay Mommy is having the baby"! Eni'yah sang. "If it's a girl can we name her LaNiyah daddy"? "K," I said and opened the door on Shontay's side/ I ran around, got in and started the truck. "La 'Real, if you don't let my baby in this truck we gone have a big problem"! I popped the locks and Eniyah got in smiling, "daddy, you funny". "Why you act like you was gone leave me"? I looked at Shontay, she mugged me and told Eniyah, "I was playing baby, daddy won't do it again, k"? "I know I'm daddy's princess"! She said laughing.

I sped off towards the hospital, as if we were in a Nascar race. "La 'Real, can you slow down before we all die"? "Oh, I was trying to get you there ASAP". "We have our whole family in here and need to be safe". "You're right baby". "Don't drive like a slug either". "Yes ma'am" . . . When we got there called I Yasmine, Sissy, Megan, Tank, my father, Jesus, Raw, BJ and Hasko. Shontay had to take my phone to keep me focused.

"Baby, breathe". She told me. "Okay, I am". I said letting out a breath. They immediately took her to a room. I went and grabbed cold water and ice cubes for her. "La 'Real, we can only do this one more time after this"! "Babe, you said four kids"! "I lied...it hurt too bad". "We can talk about that later, okay"? "Do you love me even when, I'm big and pregnant"? "Babe, how you gonna ask me that"? "Nigga, just answer the damn question, and hold my hand"!

I grabbed her hand and began to talk. "I will love you regardless of what babe, you are the brown in my family". "Okay, maybe we can do two more but that's it". I laughed and kissed her lips. "Anything. for my puzzle potna". She screamed cutting me off, "baby, it feels like it's coming now"! I pressed the doctor's button and told her "ma get help. "No baby don't leave me! I'm scared to be alone"! "Why? What's wrong"? "I'm cold and it hurts really bad" ...

I made her open her eyes and look at me, "Shontay, you

have to calm down and breathe'. "Don't be scared, I'm here with you"! The door came open and it was Sissy and Yasmine. "Go get the doctor now"! yelled. "Talk to me Shontay". "Why are you yelling baby"? "Because you're scaring me"! The doctor's rushed in and seen Shontay was ready to go into the delivery room. "She's ready John". "Get the room secured and let's go". One of them said. "Baby, don't leave". Shontay pleaded. "Never! I'm here," I said grabbing her hand. "What's wrong with her"? Yasmine asked. "Nothing, she's okay," I said looking at Yasmine crazy.

They rushed her into the labor room and spread her legs on the hoops. "Baby, did bring you some good panties for me"? "Yes babe, we did...please focus". "Ok, are you mad at me"? "No". "Push"! the doctor yelled, and she did. "Baby, it hurt so bad"! "You okay, be strong"! "Push"! He yelled again. I could see the head coming into sight, "fuck baby, can you push again"? "Yes, push again"! he yelled. She pushed the baby the rest of the way out, and we heard the baby cry. "Oww baby, it still feels like it's in there". I laughed but heard the doctor yell, "she has another one inside of there"! My face dropped, "Push"! the doctor yelled again. She pushed and out came another baby, "Damn baby, you made two, you're on pussy restriction"! She said breathing heavy. They handed us each a baby, a boy, and a girl. We named them La 'Real Jr. and Shontell.

Everybody in the room cried; not because of seeing the kids born but, for the fact the doctor who did Shontay's ultra-sound, had missed a whole other baby. That could have killed Shontay easily, being that she should have had a C-section. I handed Shontell to Sissy and went outside. First to thank the doctors, then to cry because the Lord has blessed my wife to cheat death. Stix hugged me, and he knew this time it wasn't nothing to laugh about. I had almost lost my wife! "Let it out my nigga," he said wiping his own tears off his face. "She safe now bro". "She safe" ... When I walked back in Shontay looked at me, "La 'Real, what's wrong"? I asked everybody for a minute while talked to my wife alone. They nodded and walked out the room. "Babe, the doctors said that you could have died from both kids coming out so fast... bled to death"! "You lost a lot of blood and have to be here for a lot of tests". It must not have hit her until then, and she began to cry. "It hurt so bad baby". "All I wanted to do was go to sleep". "They said when I took the panic out the ordeal, it saved yo life because you could have went into shock". She hugged me, "please don't tell nobody else". "I won't babe". "I love you and thank you for two beautiful kids". "I love you too".

Her room door came open with a bang; it was Eni'yah. "Why did I see two babies"? She said in her mean face, "instead of one"? "Whose baby is the other one"? We both laughed.

Shontay spoke up, "they are both ours". Yo sister and brother". "So, two babies were in yo tummy mommy"? "Yes, thanks to daddy". She said looking at me with the pout look on her face also. "Next time don't trick me, okay"? She said looking at us.

"Okay, we won't". I said. "Okay daddy, now what's they names and how you know which one came first"? "Your brother came first, and your sister came second. His name is La 'Real and yo sisters name is Shontell," Shontay said cutting me off and smiling, "and they are twins". "Okay, I'm not mad anymore"! "Come and give us a hug". I said, and she ran and jumped into my arms. "I love my family"! Eni'yah said. "We love you too baby". We said hugging her.

She got down and went into the hallway. I turned to Shontay, "What"? she said. "Don't ever scare me like that again". I said biting her lip. "Aw babe, I'm sorry". "You better be, because I don't know what I would have done without you"! "I'm ok," she said. "See, I told you I was happy you were here from the beginning... my angel"! "Shut up lady, I'm gonna let everybody back in to see you". "Okay King-Kong"

********NEWS FLASH********

SO MANY CATS GO TO JAIL AND TELL THEY WHOLE
LIVES TO A TOTAL STRANGER AND END UP IN DEEPER
SHT THAN WHEN THEY FIRST BEGAN.

JAIL IS THERE FOR THE CORRUPTED MINDS, BUT ALOT
IS ONLY SUCH BECAUSE INSTEAD OF FILLING OUT,
THEY WANNA FIT IN.

MOST BLACK MEN GO IN YOUNG AND COME OUT OLD.
IF THEY COME OUT, THEY COME 10 TIMES WORSE
THAN WHAT THEY STARTED AT. INSTEAD OF SEEKING
PROGRAMS THEY ARE TOO BUSY IN THE HE SAY SHE
SAY' BULLSHT, AND WANNA KEEP HAVOC AMONGST
THEY OWN PEOPLE.

 A BLACK MANS TRAIN OF THOUGHT IS STILL THAT OF A
SLAVES MENTALITY, AND HE'S FREE. ALL WE CARE

ABOUT THESE DAYS IS CARS, MONEY, DRUGS, GUNS AND HAVING SEX WITH AND DEPRIVING WOMEN... AND ANOTHER MAN'S BUSINESS.

SMALL MINDS ARE LOCAL BUT A MIND OF GLOBALNESS IS WORLDWIDE

When I left the hospital to check on my house, I noticed a few things wrong. For one, the lights were on; and I know we didn't leave in that much of a hurry, to where we left the garage open and the shed door ajar. We wasn't even in none of those places. It had been a minute since I carried a banger on me, pocket wise but I always kept a few around me in the stash. Before I crept on the house and into an ambush, I called Stix. "Hey bro, what da deal be yo"? he answered. Whispering into my phone I told him, "stock up with something nice and chunky, because my house looks like either it's been ran through or they still in that joint"! "I'll be there in a snap of the whip bro". "Don't go near the spot without me". "Okay, I'm parked down the street, left hand corner pocket". I said and dropped the line.

Who had enough William Wallace to test they brave heart or should I say nerve to shake down my spot where me and my family live. Must know God on the face-to-face basis or haven't met Satan. My phone buzzed, "Wassup Stix"? "I'm in the Range". "I see you, unlock the doors so I can slide in". "Yep," I said clicking the locks. He hopped in, "Wassup, how you wanna do this"? "Put yo hood on and rack yo hanger, we just gonna walk right up like we regular people then head to the back, secure the shed and garage, then move towards the house". "Let's go".

We hopped out, hoods on, and eased at a fast pace down the street. When we came up on the house, I spotted movement in the backyard "Yep"! We reached the back and heard the gate bang, as if somebody just hit the fence. Stix moved past me and hit the same gate. Me, I stayed in the backyard where my basement door was open. I seen movement as if whoever was on the way out spotted me, "Aye B, somebody outside in the back"! When I heard that, I opened up the cannon, two rapid shots (BOOM! BOOM). After that, I seen what looked like fire coming towards me. I had to jump in the bushes, because whatever they was shooting was fully-auto. They must have hit the side of the wall, because I had wood chips embedded in my face. "Aw fuck"! I said feeling my face burn, BOOM! BOOM! BOOM! BOOM!!! I jumped out the bushes and ran down the steps of the basement. I heard a scream like I had touched somebody, but I had to remain patient. The Fourth of July erupted outside, rapid slugs but not fully-auto. Stix, without a thought just ran through my house in a low crouch. "Who in this mufucka"? I yelled.

When I made it upstairs the front door, it was open. I reached down, and dialed Stix number. He picked up, "Aye"? "Where you at bro"? "Coming through the basement so don't shoot... I'm gonna toot when I get close". I heard "toot toot', and said, "come on bro'. "Aye nigga, whoever that was left in a burgundy Bourbon". "I chased two lil niggas and got off on them, in the truck". "The whole 30 dick... fuck bro"! Stix said looking at me, "You shot because yo face is bleeding". "I couldn't tell". "Nigga, it's a whole lot of blood on the steps". I turned every light on in the house and checked every inch. I was missing a safe, tv's, jewels and the 5.0 was gone out the garage. I hadn't drove that joint in a few years. I looked in the mirror and could see wood chips in my face. "Damn, my nigga, dats crazy". "Niggas done lost they mind about this one, promise"! "My house... my grandma had this mufucka forever, now somebody wanna come up in here, huh"? "Is, you shot"? Stix asked me. I took my shirt off and asked him do he see any holes in me. "Naw, but it looks like yo face got touched, but not penetrated"! I looked by my ear, I had a flesh wound. "Damn, that was almost my head huh"? "Nigga you Crazy"! I had a dummy safe with about five racks in it and a few letters I had written to the thief.

(IF YOU ARE READING THIS NOTE, YOU BETTER TAKE THIS MONEY AND LEAVE BECAUSE, YOU INVADED MY FAMILIES HOUSE, AND IT AIN'T BUT ONE THING THAT WILL COME YOUR WAY. :-)

"What's missing"? Stix asked. "A lil bit of nothing". Help me secure this joint and call the carpet cleaner we know". "Who, Crysis"? "Yeah, tell him to change the carpet color to black". "Yep". I walked to the shed and looked at the walls. Nobody knew, what I had stashed in here; not even Shontay. I tapped the wall and noticed it hadn't been fucked with. Then went to the garage, I found the door to the underground cellar undisturbed. They got small shit, but it was mine. The room that used to be uncle Stonez, was now a studio but it had been cleaned out and trashed... Everything gone. "We can't stay here Stix, til get to the bottom of this"! "I know" . . .

"Do y 'all' still have, the three-bedroom house available"?

"It need a few more things, but it's 97% ready". "How much y'all want for it"? "Bro, I can't charge you"! "Nigga, how much is it on the market for"? "18Ok". "2 bathrooms, upstairs, downstairs"? "Basement". "Yep, I'ma need that". "I'ma have that money to you in the morn". "Remind me to invest in real estate". "Yep,"

2 1/2 weeks later. . .

When Shontay and our twins were released, instead of going home we went to our new house in Troutdale. "Baby, whose house is this"? Shontay wanted to know. "Ours... "Why we ain't go home-home"? I hadn't told her, about the break-in and the shooting because her parents and friends were around us. When I came in the hospital and she saw my face, she flipped. "Baby, what happened to yo face, and what's the band aid for"?

"Hey babe, I missed you and love you too"! I said giving her a kiss. She caught my drift and let it go. So now that she was out, I had to tell her. "Let's get the kids settled in first, then we'll talk about everything, okay"? "Okay". "Daddy, I like our new house". Eniyah said. "It's the biggest house ever, huh"? "Yep". "Babe, who you buy this house from"? Shontay wanted to know. "You know Sissy and Stix, is on the real estate trip". "They gave you this house"? "No, I bought this house from them sweetie". "Oh". She put La 'Real Jr. down on the couch and went looking around. "Damn babe, the backyard is like a park, I see. "Go look at the closet space, and the rooms", I said smiling. "The closet is like a bedroom by itself, we could put the cribs in there and make one of the rooms for our closet". I hadn't thought of that... Maybe it was a woman thing.

"Why didn't they keep the house for themselves"? Shontay asked. "Let's put Eni'yah in the tub and order a pizza". "Okay babe". When our daughter was in the tub I started the conversation. "Babe, I was shot in the face almost, at our other house and we were robbed". "You were shot almost, and we were what"? "When you were in the hospital, someone, or people, broke into our home". "Me and Stix walked in on them doing so"! She brushed my face and felt the wood chips still under my skin.

"Oh my God, you're serious". "When we got there, they came out shooting and it turned into a big shootout". "Anybody else get hit"? "Yep, but we never found out who".

"What's missing"? "Tv's, my 5.0, jewels, safe and the whole studio". "Who would be that bold"? "I don't know yet, but my plan is to find out". "That sounds like somebody, who knew we were at the hospital" ... "I felt the same way exactly"! I had furnished the new house with everything; tv's, beds, cribs, furniture, food, clothes from the other house and cameras that record. "Let me show you something". I took her into the empty room, that the cribs were in and opened the closet. She gasped,

"Oh my God, where did you get all that from"? "I've had it since we were 17, and it grew over the years". "How much is it"? "A few million probably, I never counted it". "A What"? "You heard me". "So, that's what they were looking for at the house"? "I don't think so. You're the only one, besides me that know about it and you didn't know until now"! "Why you ain't tell me about it"? "We never needed it, with my businesses and the black card". "Why so much"? "I hustled that before quitting the drug game, when you had our daughter". "What are you going to do with it"? I went deep in the closet and showed her the wall behind the wall... "Mommy Daddy! Where are you"? Eniyah called. "In here"! We both yelled, "here we come". That's when we heard our newborn's yelling also. We smiled, "Our family is calling for us". I said. "This will take a minute to get used to, but I like it.

Make sure we call Sissy and Jamie and thank them"! "Yep. Are you ready to start in real estate"? "I can do everything from home, and anything that involves us". "What we don't know, we will find it out from the two of them. But we need to invest in something to burn that cash in the closet". "I agree, Scrooge McDuck". "Shut up" ...

Chapter 14 - The Plot Unfolds

6 Months Later. . .

I had kept my ear to the streets, about who had robbed my house in the north and took the 5.0 out the garage. In the meantime, I refurnished the house and matched the carpet with its surroundings. I changed the locks on the shed, house, added bars and got the bullets out. I wasn't gone sale my family's house. I was just gonna give it a rest, and take the valuables out, so it won't be another attempt.

6 months had passed, of trying to get the scoop on the

situation. For the first time in life, the streets wasn't talking. We had been situated in the new home and decided to invest in a lot of new things with benefits, and to wash the money. Shontay bought a building for her real estate company and called it "We All We Need". She bought a community center for the kids to go to, when school is out to help keep the youth off the streets. I bought apartments with a hundred units. I turned my studio, "My Brothaz Keepah' into a radio station, 95.3 on yo FM dial. I still owned, Strick Standardz and Sha'DayZ, the music store. Me and Stix owned a car lot together, called "Whipz'. You can get anything from old to new on our joint. I have "My Brothaz Keepah', the store, to old man Crysis so he can rinse the bad for good.

My phone rang, it was Shontay, "Hellah"? I said answering. "Babe," she said when I picked up. "Yes, beautiful". "How is the day going"? "Umm...okay". You could tell she was smiling. "And yours handsome"? "Blessed now that I've been graced with your voice".

"Glad to hear I do that to you but listen. So, I'm in traffic and tell me why I'm behind yo 5.0"? "What"? "Yep, and it's a different color with rims that's bigger . . . kinda look like a spacecraft". "How you know it's mine"? "They died the Gucci seats, but you don't think I know the car". "I seen you drive by me in, and the car you took my numbers in and the promise began"? "Where you at"? "On Alberta and 7th, going towards 15th". "Stay in yo car and kinda follow whoever... how many in the car"? "Two, they got the top dropped and the loud music playing". "I'm on Killingsworth and 15th and I'm coming to Alberta". "Babe, they just turned up 10th and parked".

"Yep, come to me, so I can see my beautiful wife". "You see me"? "Yes daddy". I pulled over, got out the car and kissed my wife through the window before I climbed in for the details of what the driver looked like. After she was done, I sent her on her way to handle business. I was in a brand-new Lex bubble, 22's, chameleon paint and tinted windows. Rolled up 10th and immediately spotted my whip, and several niggas at a white house, but in the yard, all around as if they were at a barbecue. I slowed down behind the tint and spotted a familiar face. A thick redbone named Keisha walking down the street towards the function, so I stopped. I rolled the window down a tease and asked, "is that Keisha Johnson"? She turned and said, "Yeah, who is that calling out my whole government"?

I rolled the window down the rest of the way. She walked up closer and then smiled, when she recognized me. "Is that Legend"? "Where you get this car from"? I smiled back, "I've been having this joint for a minute. "How you doing"? "I'm making it but could be doing a lot better if I was behind da wheel of something like dis"! "Material shit is for the birds, but I know where they located for yo purchase"! She smiled again, "I bet you do". "You still married to the one chick... um, um, Shontay"? "Yes ma'am, forever and a day".

"Damn, that's bad for me and unfortunate for you". "Why is that? "Stop playing, you had to know about it". "About what? "I've always thought of you as my ideal man and would have gave you a lot more to smile about". "I like to smile, but no I didn't know that you looked at me on them terms... If my memory serves me right, you use to fuck with my lil nigga and Stink, before he got killed". "I did on both". "Look, can I get in, and we talk instead of you being stopped in the street like that"? "Get in", I said and popped the locks.

She strutted past the front of my whip, so I could check out the luggage and then she got in. "Hey, it smells good in this joint, plus, you looking good". "Thanks". I said pulling off. "Whose barbecue is that"? "The nigga Relly". I searched my memory. . . Really, Really. "Who's Really"? "You mean Relly, he just got home from the fed"? "I believe he some kin, to yo boy". "My boy who"? "Hasko". "Dats what's up. Welcome home shindig, huh"? "I guess...or another hood function". "So,

145

where you working at now, and who you fuck with"? "I'm currently looking for a job and a man, if that's what you mean". "What are yo job qualifications"? "I have a G.E.D. and I know how to do everything from daycare, fast-food, hustlin, singing, wholesale talk lines, sales lady, in and out of town strapped to the dirt, desk work, to playing any position that's given... following all directions"! "All that, huh"? "And Some BOO-BOO". "What type of pay rate do you see yourself at? " Starting off"? 9-10 dollaz an hour... depend on the work, and who it is work for". "Where you live, and who you live with besides you"?

"Damn Legend, you really on yo boss up tip, huh"? "Why you say that"? "Because I feel like I'm in an interview for real, but like it because you ain't said nothing sexual and kept everything above the Skirt" I laughed, "Girl, you crazy. But it is an interview and I'm trying to see where you at in life". "For What"? "A job, of course". "Oh, is that all"? she said moving closer to me. "Absolutely"! "I live with my son in a duplex on 12th and Mason". "How much is the rent"? "Dang business... naw but I pay $725 a month, for a two bedroom and one and half bathroom". "Who you hang around, as far as females and niggaz"? "I'm a mom Legend and I don't kick it much, but I have a few home girls". "Not many men friends... oh and my baby dad is Lil Strick, he passed away now". "I know the Strick fam, and the older brother Ski-Skirt in the pen on a 10-year bid Career Criminal Shit". "I'm not sexually active at this point, because my son ain't gone just meet a new nigga all the time". "I don't get down like that"! "I respect that".

"My three home girls is Danielle, Stacy and Shelly... all women, not of the hood nature". "I believe I know Danielle". "They cool" ... "So, what was yo purpose of going to the barbecue, and looking extremely bait able"? She laughed. "I try to dress casual, but my curves are very expressive". "I see" "I was going because I seen Relly at the store, and he invited me".

"So, do you go everywhere you're invited"? "I like to eat, if you can't tell". She said, referring to the circumference of her body". "I like that 5.0. whose car is that"? "Relly's". "Dats what's up. Do you have a number, just in case you get the position"? "Yeah, and I believe I'm the most qualified for all positions because I get the job done". I smiled and took my phone out, "503-555-9951, and I can be reached anytime of the day or night"! "I can dig it...where you want me to drop you off at? Back at the Cue"?

"No, you can take me to my car. You made me realize, that all invitations can't be granted. Plus, being in the car with a real man has made me more than sweat in certain places, I rather not mention. "My bad, I didn't mean to promote that effect". "Don't apologize, that's a compliment". "I don't mean no disrespect by it". "Fo-sho that, where is yo car located"? "On 10th and Going, the Audi". "Right here"? "Yes Legend" . . ."I like that joint"! "I bet you do". "It's nice to have seen you and been in yo company". "I won't put yo conference in the streets, I know you have the wifee people". "Call me," she said reaching for a hug. "For the record, what's your sons' name"? "Josiah". "I love that name". I said.

"Why you ask that"? "Any man that you converse with, and tell him you have a child, its common courtesy he knows something out the conversation of a name, age or something". "If not, he's not a man worth you talking to". "I'ma remember that," she said shutting the car door. "Oh, what type of position is the job"? "Management". "Please call". I smiled and drove off.

So, what I got out the whole conversation was that, Hasko's cousin got my car and he may be involved. I picked up the phone and dialed Shontay's number, "Hello"? she answered. "Babe" ... I couldn't even get the words out". "Huh? What happened"? "You member the Keisha Johnson, the chick we went to school with"? "Yes". The thick light-skinned, pretty chick"? "Yes, well seen her when I hit the block. she gave me all the info I needed". "She just walked up talking"? "Naw babe, I told her I knew of a management position at some apartments, and then she told me who car it was". "Whose apartments"?

"Mine's... and the nigga Hasko mixed up in this shit". "Oh...La 'Real don't get fucked up, being sneaky though"! "I won't". She hung up. I called Stix and told him, I was on my way to the dealership and that we needed to discuss developments in the 5.0 ordeal.

When I walked in, Stix was on the phone. "Aye mom, I'ma call you back and Swing by on you and the girls" ... "Ok, tell lil sis I'll be over there". "I wanna talk to her about this guy thing... Ok, I love you too". He turned to me, "wassup bro"? "Man, trying to figure out the real my nig". "How's mom and sisn'em doing"? "Lil sis got a boyfriend, who apparently has a hand problem". "May have to tighten the lil nigga up a taste". "Word, I can see that, but on the house, being robbed gig, Hasko sound real fishy like"! "Call the nigga and see where he at". "He may be at the barbecue thing". "We need more finesse than just that, but fuck it, call the nigga"! "I'm on that right now", Stix said phone ringing already on speakerphone. "Hello"? Hasko said when he picked up. "Wassup Hasko"?

"Shit, at my cousin barbecue on 10th and Alberta"! "Who cue is that"? "My cousin Relly, just touched bout a month ago". "Yeah, dig dat, so it's live over there"? "Hell yeah, it's major my nigga". "Y 'all welcome to come if you want"! "I'ma call Legend and see if he wanna slide by there with me, if that's cool"? "If all my niggas ain't invited, I'm never gonna be here myself". "Call me when you get here so I can walk y 'all in, will do". The line dropped. "That nigga sound suspect to me bro". "Yeah, I heard". I said, thinking. "Nigga, let's slide through that joint to see what we can see". "Yep, gotcho thunder cat"? "You know it... never leave home without it"!

We jumped in Stix '06 Charger on 24's and smashed the whip to the cue. It had gotten bigger since the ride-by earlier. You had niggas from the Murda Block, Woodlawn, Lop, Unthank, GD, Tha Mobb, and a gang of hood-rats, prep jerks, and others. We stepped out the jet, on the runway and ran right into Hasko. "Hey"! he said when he bumped into Stix, not looking. Then when he turned around and saw us, he smiled, and threw his hands out to embrace us. "Wassup my niggas"? "Hasko Hasmatic, what it do"? I said. "Wassup boy"? Stix threw in. "What it look like in this joint"? "Man, just a hood function, with good food". "Let me introduce y 'all to my aunt, and cousin. Relly"! he yelled. A nigga walked up about

190lbs., long hair, a few tats, copper complexion skin tone and about 5'11" with jewels and a big ass medallion. (None of which were mine.) "What's up Hasko"? He said.

"Aye, these my niggas cudn"! "Legend," I said reaching to shake his hand. "Stix homie, welcome to the free world". "Nice to meet real niggas blood". "Y 'all welcome to anything, round this camp". He told us. "Yep" "Where you do your bid at"? I asked him. "I just touched from da feds". "I did my time in USP's but paroled from Sheridan after four and a half". I reached in my pocket and tossed the nigga a rack. "Welcome back to civilization". "Hopefully this where you remain, after that shit you been through"! He embraced me and told me he liked the Legend nigga already. I smiled and walked off with Stix and Hasko at my side. "Where is yo aunt at my nig"? I asked Hasko. "She in here . . . Auntie Eva! These are my potnas right here, Stix and Legend". He introduced as she was walking up.

"Why can't men have regular names these days Eddie"? Hi, I'm hit Aunt Eva and you are"? She said holding her hand out. "I'm La 'Real". I said shaking her hand. "And I'm Jamie". Stix said cutting me off and shaking her hand. "How y 'all doing"? "Y 'all smoke weed"? "Yes ma'am". Stix said. "No "ma'am". "Just Aunt Eva". She said handing us a blunt. "Dats killa bud, y 'all enjoy yo self and be careful". "You too Aunt Eva, and thanks".

The barbecue was jumping, til my phone rang, "Hellah"? I answered. "Where you at"? Shontay asked. "At the barbecue, me and Stix". "Oh, I was just making sure you were safe. I'ma let you get back to mingling". "You need to cut that out babe and stop acting lefty when you pitch right". That's when I noticed, I was talking to myself and she had hung up already. When did we start hanging up on each other and shit? (I asked myself) Stix and I grabbed a plate, and stayed for another hour or so, til a female fight broke out. A little nigga walked in the cue, hugged up with another chick and didn't realize his live-in baby mama was there. It was comedy for the young dude... He blasted a few jokes off and was met by a drink and a slap, and that's when the fight started.

We left, and I told Stix I didn't see the fishy business. He said, "I did bro, but not with Hasko"! "The Relly nigga left from by us and the Unthank nigga he went by him and whispered in his ear, then he turned around and looked back in our direction". "Which nigga"? I wanted to know. "The Snake nigga". "Oh yeah" ... "I noticed a lil nigga they was with, had an apparent gunshot wound to the stomach, because he was showing a few bitches like he was 2Pac" ... The blood in the basement! "Oh, and did you hear where the nigga paroled from"? "Yep" ... Then we both said, "Magnify" at the same time.

Chapter 15 - Insecurities

When I stepped in my house I could hear my kids and my wife. She was on the phone cussing and they were either waking up or going to sleep. "Yeah girl, a barbecue, and I'm at home with the kids"! When I walked in the room, she froze as if she had seen a ghost. "Aye, yas, I'ma call you back, ok"? I smiled, "did you wanna discuss something with me, before you slandered me as if I'm a bad daddy and husband"? "Ummm" . . .Must have looked like a demon, because that's all she could say before the twins started crying. "Don't worry", I said holding my hand out to stop her. "Let me go get them, since I ain't been doing my daddy thing, too busy at functions and shit". I walked to tend to the kids, and heard her call for me but I kept walking…

I had never seen my wife act like this, so my way of getting back at her was to stay away while under the same roof. I knew she had a little baby fat but, I didn't know she had started feeling as if she didn't appeal to me anymore. I had never cheated on Shontay, nor exercised the thought to do so; but I didn't like being salted for shit I wasn't doing. We would lay in the bed, and it felt as if the split was in the middle of us. We hadn't really talked or touched sexually... Our sex life when all was good, it was like three times a day shit... Not counting the double sessions, with the oral business. I missed her touch and the way we vibe, but I didn't cause this situation with her insecurities. It had us in a bad space. It was up to her, to fix us. As my wife, she owed me an explanation; as to what was wrong and trust what she vowed to have when she said, "I do".

When a woman has kids, and a man is not present for most of the day, a woman begins to either feel trapped, lonely or have thoughts of infidelity.

This is how a woman shakes off the man, they are involved with. By accidental blaming, distance, lack of attention, talk on the phone about you when you arrive, refer to the kids as just her kids, food not cooked even for the kids, the split in the bed, no communication, from no panties to granny panties, fake sleeping, gone all day and speaking with the head low as if they don't respect you enough to look you in the face.

(A lot of females lose the confidence they had when y 'all met and to regain it, they disrespect themselves and the man they are involved with. Some dress like trash, throw themselves at every man, commit adultery, or just lose the class that made them appealing in the beginning... not to say this happened in my story, I just had to go in on the best women who go below they standards for no apparent reason).

Anyways, we hadn't been on the regular with our love life, and I felt like maybe one of us needed a breather. When she went in the bathroom to take a bath, I heard the water start and wanted to make sure I didn't invade on her privacy, so I knocked on the door. "Come in", I heard her say through the door. I watched her cover up when I came in, which has never been a part of our marriage. "Is there something you need me to do, or something you need to do tonight"? "No, why"? "I'ma go to the studio and record a few songs". "Okay, that's fine". "I'm not going anywhere La 'Real". She said looking at the wall.

I nudged her head and lifted her chin up. "When I married you, you talked with yo chin and head up". "Why look at the ground now"? I asked her. She didn't respond. "Shontay," I said, and for the first time in days she looked at me directly with those honey-brown eyes. "Do you hear me talking to you"? I saw her eyes cloud up and the tears fall out, "Yes Legend, I hear you". I was shocked when I heard the name fall off her tongue, because she had never referred to me as my street name. "So, that's who I am to you now"? "Legend"? She didn't answer, just tears...I got up to leave, but when I was almost pass her she grabbed my hand. "No, please don't leave La 'Real. I'm sorry". I turned and looked at her and watched as everything poured out within her. "I'm lonely, I miss yo touch, yo smile, the way you look at me, the way you make me feel as a woman, my husband, yo body heat and the way you make love to me". She said and put her head down!

"I miss my puzzle piece that completes me, my best friend, my wife, the trust, yo body, my family, and the woman who graduated with a bachelors, and gave me three beautiful kids. The confident woman, who owns a successful business. The woman who could have given her virginity to any man but chose to save and share it with me". I leaned down and kissed her tears. "Babe, I didn't take yo innocence, you gave it to me, with yo heart to cherish and protect . . . and as far as that protector I swore to be when I said, "I Do" to you! Money has never made me happy, nor material things... Being yo husband and a daddy, is all my life consist of, and secures who I am as a man. I love everything I have with you! You hurt me the other day, when I came in the house and heard what you said on the phone about me, as if I was a dead-beat daddy and husband".

"Then today, you call me a name that you have never once acknowledged, in the 20 years we've known one another". She tried to drop her head, but I told her, "don't you dare drop yo head on me again"! "I would rather you turned yo back and walked away from me"! She looked back at me.

I let my hand drop and gave her enough time, to think about what I said and went to lay down taking all my clothes off.

(IN MEN'S CASES LEAVING WOULD MOST DEFINITELY DESTROY THE RELATIONSHIP, EVEN THOUGH YOU AINT IN THE WRONG, LEAVING CAN NEVER BE RIGHT).

She remained in the bathroom, for about ten more minutes and when she came out she carried a wet towel in her hand. "La 'Real "... I looked up at her, "yes Shontay"? "Can I lay next to you, and you wipe away my insecurities with this towel" ..." Tell me we gone be okay, and that you love me and only me" ... "Then kiss my eyes again and hold me in yo arms". She was looking me in my eyes... I stood up and grabbed her hand, and took her back in the bathroom, in which she had just came out of, and walked her in front of the mirror. (Which was almost a full-body mirror) "Look into the mirror". I said and. When I said that, I began to undress her, while she watched me watch her. I never took my eyes off her and began to talk to her through the mirror. "Nothing you see in this reflection, can hurt who you are". "Within my heart and to me, everything you see now is our reality". "The reason you see yo reflection first, is because that's how I see me through you, yo reflection is also mine". "I see you, before I see myself". "The reason you see me behind you is because, I'm that backbone a man that completes you". "In this same order, is how it will always be, for the fact a King's castle is nothing without a Queen". "Your beauty is not what makes me love you Shontay". "You being the root to my family, and completing me within is what makes you, you".

A lot of women break down and listen to insecurities but baby, you've made it... you've made it". She was butt naked, head lifted and tears streaming. I rubbed my hands all over her body, while she was lost in my stare and touch. "I love you Shontay. I promise to always love you for eternity". She blinked and tried to catch her tears, but I said, "No, let them fall...get it all out in front of me, so I will know what yo pain looks like". "When you hurt, I also hurt because it is you who makes me well when I feel sick". "I'm here and there's nowhere else, I would rather be than with you when you need me to be". "I am yo husband". I reached for the shower and turned it on a little bit hotter than warm. I took my eyes off my wife and stepped in the shower in the back and reached for her, "Come here baby, get in the shower with me"!

She reached for my hand and got in, turning towards the nozzle in which I spun her to face me. "No, I wanna look at you. I took the towel out her hand and grabbed the soap. "I won't just wash yo face baby, I'll wash yo whole body". She hugged me and held onto me while I washed her hair, her back, her private box, her breasts, her ass, and then I got on my hands and knees and washed her legs and feet. A lot of soap everywhere! When I stood up and put her under the nozzle, I followed the water with my kisses, not sexually but to let her know she was my Queen. "LA "Real"? "Yes babe"? "Thank you for not leaving, I needed you more than you'll ever know". "I missed you a lot mommy... "Why would I ever leave you"? "I don't know but it's my greatest fear". "I would rather not live, if my living is without you"! "I was conceived, standing up and I'm gonna die and man up in the same fashion"! "I called you Legend to get yo attention, not to disrespect you". "It's okay baby, I'm not mad at you". "Promise"? "Promise," I said kissing her nose, mouth and then her eyes. "Let me get you out this shower and dried off before you get sick". I turned the water off, reached for the big towel and dried my wife off. I took her in the room, turned the heat on for a few, and lotioned and massaged her body until she fell asleep.

I got up to check on my daughter Eniyah and made sure the house was locked up. I allowed my wife to sleep, being that she had been up and ain't slept in a few days. I had been lying there staring at her for hours.... she was spread out butt naked, on the bed and finally finding rest when I began to touch and taste. At first, she didn't wake up, but when she did, it was with a moan. "Mmmm, baby please don't ever stop". I made her rise to where explosions begin with no end. I engaged her in 'I miss you sex", instead of "make-up sex'.

WORD TO THE WISE: NEVER SOLVE A PROBLEM WITH SEX BECAUSE WORDS CURE, NOT PUSHING AND POKING. ONCE SEX IS OVER, NOTHING IS SOLVED.

MEN DON'T ALLOW YO PRIDE, TO CAUSE YOU TO LOSE SOMETHING SPECIAL. ONCE YOU ALLOW A BREATHER OR SPLIT IN THE BED, YOU ALLOW NONSENSE IN YO RELATIONSHIP.

YOU NEED TO PUSH YO SHADOW ASIDE AND KEEP THE BEST REFLECTION SOLID. A WOMAN'S WORTH IS VERY IMPORTANT TO A MAN, BECAUSE WHEN HE FALLS WEAK, SHE WILL BE STRONG FOR THE BOTH OF YOU).

Chapter 16 - Whiplashed

I hadn't been focused, the day of the barbecue because of the way Shontay was behaving and that was very dangerous; to be in the field with my mind clogged. When I finally got out, me and my wife had an understanding. So, I went to check on the apartment buildings progress. I had bought them from previous owners, instead of building them myself. I had weeded out the bad seeds, to run the shit business like, instead of the hood type. I called the Keisha Johnson chick, "Hello"? she answered. "Hello. May 1 speak to Ms. Keisha Johnson"? "Speaking". "How you doing"? "I'm okay" ... She said, not knowing who she was talking to. "Well, I'm calling for the job you interviewed for". "Legend"? "No ma'am, La 'Real Sykes". "Hi La 'Real". "Hey, when do you think I can meet with you, concerning the conversation we had"? "I'm available now. If you like, you can come over to my house". "I don't think that would be appropriate, being that I have a wife and although I'm in control, what those don't see will hurt at thought... so I would prefer you to meet me at the apartments on Stark and 176th, they're called the Legions".

"Where will I find you"? "In the Office". "Okay, can you give me like 20 minutes, so I can drop Josiah off"? "Bring him too, if you like. The owner won't mind, I'm sure". "Ok, I'm on my way". "That will be just fine". I said and hung up.

(For the readers, get your minds out the gutter Dis Legend, not a cream-puff or fuckboy. The little nigga Strick was killed in a drug transaction gone bad and I'm the one who sent him to get the money and had never really did nothing for his family to repay them for having my hands in what happened. I mean, I paid for the funeral, and when his brother touch I'ma hold him down a great job position in one of my establishments. So, no don't wanna fuck Keisha. My word is all live and die for).

She arrived 15 minutes after the call, knocked on my office door with her son in hand. I opened the door and to her surprise, we were alone. "Hey Legend". "La 'Real, please". "Okay, La 'Real, where is the owner and what am I supposed to do"? "Do you believe you can manage these, if it was put in yo hands to do so"? And not be hood with how you conduct yourself"? "Stop playing La 'Real". "Do you think the owner will like me"? "Keisha, I am the owner"! I said. Her eyes popped open, "All of these"?

"Yes ma'am, plus a few. Now, can you answer my question"? "Yes, um, sir. I do believe I can manage these apartments". I reached over and held my hand out for her son to slap it, "Hey lil man". He smiled and gave me five. "Okay, let me get a few things straight with you, and give you a better understanding professionally". "I respect my wife for number

1, so by no means is my help to journey inside of yo clothes"! "For two, I knew yo son's dad and he made an impact on my life, which I respect". "Three, as my employee you are to run my establishment like a business, and respect what's mine". "If you need security, I will provide such, but by no means are you to cut breaks". "Do not give any type of deals, with my apartments". All that, "Hey girl, you can get you a spot"! "No". Please screen all tenants thoroughly and keep this place safe for lil man and all the others who live here". I grabbed a key and told her to follow me.

We walked up to the door of an apartment and opened it up. "Would you like to look inside"? "Yes, if you don't mind". She walked in the door, "Why this one already got furniture inside and everything else to furnish it"? "It's finished for you and handed her the keys". "This apartment's rent is $750, but for you and your son it's free". "You will be paid $50 a day and receive checks every two weeks". "Oh, and the phone is in the company name, which is already on". "The number is on the receiver". Then I went in my pocket and handed her the first check for $750. "This apartment you giving me, with new furniture, food, tv's and everything else in it"?

"Welcome, to Legion's Keisha". "Congrats on your accomplishments". "I've never had nobody in life, do what you've done for me". "How can I ever repay you"? "By running my establishment right, as I asked you to, and getting yo life together for you and my potnas son". She went to hug me, but I shook her hand instead. "It's a PlayStation 2 in his room, and please do me a favor and not mention to anybody what came with yo job". "I did this to help, not poke". So, don't bite the hand, that feeds you". I said smiling. "I understand Mr. Sykes and will respect yo wishes". "Thank you". I said and walked out of the apartment. "Um, how will reach you if need be"? "I know yo number . . . member, it's my business to know". "You shouldn't have any problems though, everything in here is new". "Oh, and that Lex bubble is for sale, at the car lot called Whips". We do trade-in and down payments," I smiled and left.

I called to check on my wife and kids, "Hello"? I heard the beautiful voice come over the phone. "Hey sexy, what you doing"? "Just finished looking at the building, for the Legacy Village project". "What it look like"? "It's almost ready for the kids and the adults. A daycare, job readiness classes, parenting, big brother and sister program and a domestic abuse prevention aid". "Damn babe, you got everything but a bible class". "Shut up! How is yo day going"? "Great, now that I see my wife, is active and proud of her accomplishments".

"How's yo day"? She laughed, "I think I may be a little horny after hearing yo voice"! "Describe the meaning you speak of". "500 degrees and slippery, with icing on it like ice cream". "Put yo finger in and tell me the color of the juice". "Ummm... silky cream complexion, like lotion". "Kids"? "Both in they cribs, the other daycare".

"Why do I wanna have phone sex, with the woman on the other end of this phone"? "Probably because my whole aura is sexy and maybe because you're a nasty caller". "Where you at in the house"? "I'm laying in daddy's bed with everything off". "When did you strip"? "As soon as you indicated, I turned you on". "I like when you read my mind". "Mm mm, it's even juicier". "How are yo legs positioned"? "On the wall daddy".

I turned into my driveway and stepped out the car, "You rubbing it fo yo, husband"? "Yes baby, I am". "Is yo eyes closed"? "Yes... " she moaned. "Put yo finger inside of there and let me hear yo pussy talk on the phone". I walked in my house and stripped by the door. She put her pussy to the phone and could hear how wet she was, "Baby, you hear it"?

"Yep, make it cum for me. I'ma listen to you okay"? "Okay". I walked up the stairs, "Oh shit baby, I'm so fuckin wet". "Shut yo eyes and make it cum for me"! "Oh, oh, shit baby! I love being freaky for you"! I watched her, playing with the pussy and my dick got rock hard, from how she worked it. "I'm finna cum right now and it's big"! She started to squirt, "Oh my God baby, it's coming out like a waterfall"! "I can see it". Her eyes popped open, and it look like she started to cum even harder, fingers never stopped moving. I walked to the bed and just put my dick inside and licked her fingers clean. "Yes...oh, I'm cumming!"! She said grabbing her hair. I pounded the pussy in rapid succession, left for two pumps, right for three, the straight for five, "Yes baby, put yo name on it, it's yo pussy". I lifted her legs above her head and grinded in the pussy, "ow baby you tryna make more kids"! "No, I'm just being nasty with my wife"! I pushed and grinded and she lost it and began to shake like Elvis. I pulled out and watched the cum coming out, "I can't control it baby"! I pushed back in hard and pumped ten fast ones and took it back out. The scream that she let out woke up both babies, and it waterfalled. "baaaaby"! She breathed harder and her body shook like she was having a seizure.

She grabbed a pillow and covered her face. I put it back in and slow-stroked her, taking the pillow off her face and kissed her moans. "Oh, I wanna feel yo cum daddy. Cum inside my pussy daddy" Eight pumps later I was starting to cum... instead of cumming all in her, I let some of it go inside then pulled it out and came on her stomach and titties. "Wipe it all over daddy. "Why you didn't just stay inside me", because you were guaranteed to be pregnant". "Why you didn't tell me, you were watching me"! "Because you made my fantasy, go great and you didn't need to know" ... "I came real hard when, I looked, and you were here". "I don't think you've ever made this happen to me". I blew on her nipple and felt the shakes coming from her body. "I'm still cummin baby". "I know, let me get these two bottles". "Okay". When I got up, the whole bed cover was wet. I smiled and went to the kitchen for the bottles. When returned Shontay was still shaking but asleep. I positioned both bottles and lay down next to my wife. "I love you beautiful". "I love you too" ... she said snuggling up against me. I kissed her head and took a nap also.

Must have overslept because when I woke up, both twins was next to me in the bed and I smelled food being cooked. I could also hear Eni'yah singing along, with the Little Mermaid movie. My phone was buzzing from all the missed calls. I searched and seen a call from Stix, Tank, Hasko, Sissy and a few blocked numbers. I picked up my phone and called Shontay. "Hey sleepy head, what's up"? She said when she answered. "I woke up and you was gone". I said pouting. "Not far away babe, just making food for my family is all"! "How you feel"? "Like you took my soul...are you the devil"? "Nope, I'm the husband"!

"Damn, I'm for real though babe. You've never did me like that...what happened to you"? "Watching you touch yo self-sparked the demon in me" ... "Oh, it scared me, because I couldn't stop cumming and even now it's sensitive". "You turn me on, but I'm not sorry bout it". "Don't be, I loved the performance. Yo phone kept ringing, but I didn't pick it up and Sissy called me, but I didn't make it to my phone in time".

"What are you cooking"? "The taco's, duh". We both laughed. "Send my princess in here". "Don't forget you naked". "Oh yeah, where my clothes at"? "They were by the door, creeper". She said smiling. "Oh, we need to change the blankets. They were black, now they're black and white"! "Shut up, you made me do it"! "Maybe...but the whole blanket"? "It wouldn't stop". "So, I broke it then"? "Nah, it works splendid". "I bet...send my baby to me". "Okay daddy". I heard the stairs and the footsteps, then the door opened. "Daddy, are you awaked now"?

I faked sleep and my door shut back. I heard pouty footsteps and then my phone buzzed. "Babe, why this girl got her sad face on? "Like my daddy still sleep?'" Shontay asked me. "Send her back up here, and tell her to wake me up, she gotta give me a kiss". "Okay". I hear steps, then the door opens again. She walked over to me and said, "Daddy, are you awaked"? I didn't move, then she leaned over and kissed me. I twinkled my eyes and said, "You've awakened me my princess"! She smiled, "I waked you up"?

"Yep. Only a kiss from a princess can do it"! "Only mine? Me"? She said pointing at herself. "Only you Princess Eniyah Marie"! "Oh, I didn't know it worked on daddies".

"Only on daddies because I'm the only man you should kiss now...right"? "Yep. Right"! "How was yo day beautiful"? "Fine...did you miss me"? "Yep, and our babies and mommy". Give me a hug". She reached and hugged me tight and kissed me again. "I love you Eni'yah". "I love you too daddy". "How much"? "Dis many". She said stretching her arms out as wide as they went. "That's the most, in the world ever". "Yep". I smiled and told her to go and see if mommy was done with our tacos. "Okay daddy, and my movie on".

"Okay baby, go watch yo movie". When she left out I reached for two diapers, so I could change my babies. They were getting big. Shontell was the quiet one and La 'Real Jr. was the stuck-up one. I pushed in the bathroom, to relieve myself and wash my face. My phone buzzed, "Hellah"?

170

I answered.

Chapter 17 - Detailz

"Yeah, what's up with you bro"? Sissy said. "What's up Sissy"? "Damn, Shontay must have put that thang on you boy"? "Shut up Sissy, you know I'm the champ". "Self-proclaimed, but unannounced . . . anyways, I've been calling to see if you heard about BQ"? "About the little time he got"? "Nah, about him getting killed in Walla, Walla" "Hell naw, I ain't heard no bullshit like that. Who told you that shit"? "The channel 12 news" . . . "What they say happen"? "He was fighting a dude on the breezeway, and stomping dude, the police dude from the tower ordered him to stop but he didn't, so they shot him".

"Wow! That's mind-blowing they killed him instead of wounding him". "Yep, I agree" . . . "Anybody talk to Angie"? "She ain't been picking up her phone"! "When I get out and about, I'll slide over there to see what's up with her. Where yo husband"? "In the living room drinking, talking about fuck da police. You wanna talk to him"? "I'll call him back after I eat with my family. "Okay champ don't get to acting negative like yo boy in the other room". "I love you and enjoy yo meal...what she is making anyway"? "I love you too Sissy, and she's making tacos". "Boy, you just may be the champ". She said laughing. "Bye" . . .

When Shontay came upstairs to bring me my plate, I smiled and kissed her eye-lids out of gratitude for her cooking. "Thank you, beautiful queen of mine". She smiled and said, "Whatever you like". In her Coming to America voice. "Aye babe, did you hear about BQ"? "What do you mean baby"? "Turn to the news". I said looking at my watch. "It's almost five o'clock". "What happen"? As soon as she turned it on they were talking about it...

A man was shot and killed after a fight in the Washington State Penitentiary has been identified as Bryant Quintell of Portland, Oregon... Investigators say that, Quintell engaged in a fight and repeatedly stomped on another inmate's head. After being told to stop and get on the ground, the officer of the north tower fired, when they seen no compliance. Investigators are looking into this matter, and until everything is looked at, the Washington State Penitentiary remains on lockdown and officers are on paid leave...Peter Williams, News 12

"Damn, my nigga dead". "Yeah, that's sad. I wonder why he didn't stop". "You know BQ do something, he go all the way". "Yeah, I'ma call Angie and see if her and the kids need anything". "Can we eat before you do that, Queen"? "Of course, daddy, you earned that meal, plus some". She said shaking as if she was cold. "Really"? "Really"...

After my shower and meal, I went into the magic closet and grabbed some doe out for my niggas family. In my head I kept thinking, in the end bro died trying to be slick with the Dynasty chick. He had no reason to contact that lady after what we did. One false move got a nigga killed. Rather you die that day, or later...death remains in your back-yard waiting.! I stopped by Angie's house, and was greeted by a light-skinned nigga after knocking. "Wassup playboy"? He said. "Aye, is Angie here"? I asked him. "Yeah, who is you"? My first thought was to ask the nigga who he was, but I didn't. "I'm L" "Aye Angie, some nigga name L is at yo door"! "Let him in, that's like my brother"! I heard her call from inside the house. "Oh". She came to the door and said, "Come in bro". "And you are"? I finally asked the light-skinned nigga. "I'm

Classic". He answered. "Dats what's up". "Hey Legend, wassup bro"? Angie said.

I could tell she had been sniffing drugs due to the residue on her nose. "Shit, came over here to see if you and the kids were okay". "Why wouldn't we be"? I looked at the Classic cat and asked him if I could please speak to Angie in private. "Yeah dog, you got that". 'I'ma be back here Angie". He said walking through the house. "K, make yoself comfortable Classic". She told him, then turned to me. "What's wrong bro"?

"You don't know about BQ" "I ain't fucking with that nigga bro". "He was fucking on my friend Tasha!" "Yeah, but you gotta put that to the side for this". "What, he sent you over here, because I ain't picked his phone calls up"? "Naw. ...Angie, BQ was killed today in Walla Walla during a fight"! "Whatchu mean killed"? "The police shot him, because he wouldn't stop fighting". "Legend, he just called last night...how he dead"? "Turn on the tv and watch the news". "Is the kids here"? "Will you be okay"? "No, the kids at my mom's house and you tell BQ since he wanna fake dead for my attention not to call me"! "Angie, are you on something"? "No, why you say that"? Just then, the Classic nigga came out with the plate, "Angie put more on the plate"!

Before I knew what, I was doing, I slapped the plate in the niggas face and took off on him twice, "Get yo bitch ass out my homeboys' house"! "Angie, get this nigga off me, before I clean his carpet"! "Legend, stop! "Please stop...it's okay". "Who is this nigga Angie"? I asked. "He's my dude Legend". "Please stop". "Nigga, don't ever in yo life disrespect the Legend like dat, passing my sis some dope". "Cudn, dis my bitch and dis what we do in our space". I got off him and he got up. "Nigga neva rack back on Classic, den let me up". He threw the plate, which I easily side stepped, but he caught me with an overhand left. BAM, I staggered back to regain my composure and caught a right. "Nigga, I ain't no pussy". "I'm da truth at this shit". Classic said. I shook off the two and went south-paw on this nigga. "I like that nigga...now I'm gone punish you bitch"!

He swung, I side-stepped and served the whopper with cheese meal, catching him on stagger. "Ahh, bitch ass nigga". He said rushing me. We start tussling tough... He went for the trip and moved my leg and I dumped him. "Play time over bitch"! I said and unleashed the nite-nite medicine. "Stop Legend, y'all tearing up my house"! By then, I touched that chin and felt him go limp. "Go to sleep bitch ass nigga"! Nite nite"! I didn't stomp the nigga, but in my mind, I'm thinking, "this bitch ass nigga tried to steal me like second base or somethin got up and made my way to the door. "Watch the news," I said leaving the house. Before I made it to the car, I heard POP POP POP. I ducked, but realized I was hit.

"Bitch ass nigga wassup now"? Classic yelled from the doorway shooting. I slid in my whip and grabbed my stash box, reaching fast seeing Classic run towards the car. "Ain't no escape now nigga", Classic screamed running up on the car. I opened, BOOM! BOOM! BOOM! BOOM! BOOM! "Yeah nigga! What now?"!

He slid behind a parked car but fired two more times. POP POP. One of them hit my car... I just jumped out the car in full sprint towards him busting. BOOM! BOOM! BOOM! BOOM! BOOM! I heard him let out a grunt. "Bring yo ass out nigga"! "Dis what you wanted bitch"? "Legend no"! "Please no"! Angie screamed. "He's down"! I tried to get closer, but he got off again. "You gone have to kill me"! He screamed, letting off four more rounds... all hitting the metal of somebody car...before I heard a click. "Aww bitch" You done fucked up now dats what you want, huh"? I yelled out, running up on him to finish this shit. Angie ran and stood over him and snatched the gun. "No Classic baby, you need medical attention"!

I ran directly over to him, heat aimed, ready to finish the

nigga off" ...No Legend, you need medical too! Get out of here before the police come"! I looked at the nigga and told him, "even demons can get a blessing from God". I heard the sirens coming, I ran and jumped in my car and got out of there.

Dialing Sissy's number, it rang, "Hello"? I heard her answer. "Sissy, I'm shot"! She screamed, "Where you at bro"? "I'm on the... um... freeway heading toward Vancouver". "Where you hit at"? "Everywhere it feel like" ... "Pull over and call for some help"! "No! The guy who shot me, is also shot and I gotta get this gun off me and in the water". I swerved. "Oh my God bro, you okay"? "No Sissy, I told you I feel like I'm shot everywhere"! I mashed the breaks and got out on the bridge. "Where you at bro"? "I'm on the bridge... I just got rid of everything". "Stay there"! "No, I gotta get" ... "Bro, bro".

Everything went black, and from there I only heard voices, but I didn't understand. "Get up La'reeeal"! "Oh my God"! "No, La 'Real! My eyes cleared, and I snatched the phone. "He...hellah" "Bro, we see yo car". "Where you at"? Before I could answer, I felt hands and seen Stix face . . . then I blacked out. I woke up to two hands inside mine and mumbles... When my eyes opened Sissy and Shontay held both my hands. I groaned from the pain in my stomach. "Don't try to speak bro, you're in the hospital". I tried to speak anyway, and noticed the tube in my mouth. "It's okay baby, I'm here". Shontay said.

I pointed at the tube, and my wife called the doctor. "Excuse me sir, can you take the tube from his throat"? He walked over and took it out. "There you are" ... "Thank you". Shontay told him. "Sissy, put some water to my mouth". I said. "Here, drink". "I did, thank you Sissy". She smiled at me. "What happened babe and why did you have 20 thousand cash on you"? I had forgot that I went to take Angie the money for her and her kids. "Angie boyfriend and I got into it"! "What"? Stix said, talking for the first time. "I went over there to see if she was okay, and the nigga came out with drugs, so I rocked him terribly". "Yeah, it looks like you been in a fight". "She ain't even know about BQ. . .she was too high to figure out what I was tryin to tell her". "She didn't already know"? "No, and the nigga was disrespectful"! "Who was the nigga bro"? "Some bitch ass nigga name Classic"! "I'ma call this bitch and see what's up". Shontay cut in. "No babe!" "You gotta get me outta here 'Scoob'". I said, trying to get myself together. "Bro, you're not going anywhere". Sissy said. "Why not Sissy"? "You got four bullets in yo body boy, you ain't 2Pac". "Four shots couldn't kill me, I took it and smiled"! I said being funny, then I asked. "Four shots for real"? Damn, where I get shot at"? "Um, in yo back, chest, shoulder and stomach". Sissy told me. "Damn, the Classic nigga with the shit and got aim huh"? "Babe, dats not funny". Shontay said getting in her feelings. "Okay, I won't laugh, but Angie saved the niggas life... she on dope bad though". "Dats why she ain't pick up"? Shontay said, and right then her phone rang, "Dis da bitch Angie right here"! Pointing at her phone and putting it on speaker when she answered. "Hello"? "Hi Shontay". We heard Angie's voice on the other end. "Hello Angie". "How is he"? "Fucked up"! "How the fuck you think he is"? "So is Classic, he got shot four times"! "So", Shontay told her with an attitude. "I didn't believe bro, when he said BQ was dead, but I see he was telling the truth"! "Who would play about some shit like that"? . . . "He came to check on you and the kids". "I know now... I'm sorry he had to see me like that". "Tell him I got rid of the thing and gave the police a different account of what happened". "You didn't mention my husband, did you"? "Not at all neither of us did".

"Dats cool... so how you dealing with the BQ thing"? "I'm not, I'm dealing with what happened at my house". I reached for the phone, "Angie, who is that nigga"? "Legend, leave that alone". "He lost a lung and have to wear a colostomy bag". "You ain't tell the nigga nothing bout me"? "I wouldn't do that, you've always been like a brother to me and good to my family". "Okay, we need to bury BQ and it's a must, that dude ain't around when we do". "He still gone be in the hospital, he's really hurt"! "Okay, I'ma have Shontay or Sissy call you". "I'm glad you okay, and I'm sorry you had to see me like that". "Get help before it's too late". "I will" ... and the line dropped. "Da nigga fucked up"! "He gotta wear a shit bag"! I said smiling.

Everybody looked at me, and the smile left my face. I looked down and for the first time I noticed the bag on me, "Really"? "How long I gotta have this shit?"!? "4-8 weeks". Sissy answered me. "Fuck! "Just when I had the mufuckin belt". "We are not having sex at this point, I am not putting my belt up on the line". "You just can't take a niggas championship like dat". "Dis man shot, and he still talkin bout the damn championship belt". "Shontay, what you do to my brother"? "Gave him my innocence and married him". "I see"! Sissy said.

Three days inside a hospital will drive a nigga nuts... Sissy told me the whole story of how Stix found me on the ground by the bridge and had picked me up crying. "Bro, stay with me"! Sissy said imitating, the hoe ass voice he used.

"Jamie, don't be ashamed now, I cried with you, member"? Sissy finished with a smile. "The whole time, all you kept mumbling bout was Shontay gone be mad", Stix said. I smiled, "who called her"? "I did", Stix said, "and boy was she mad"! We all laughed. "I drove yo car here full of blood and bullet holes everywhere". "Where my car at now"? "I took it to the cleaners and got the holes filled in, plus took the shells from the inside, out myself". A knock came to the door and we all looked, "Um, come in". Shontay called out. Damn, it was the preacher... my pops! "Good evening everybody". "Good evening". We all said. "How you feeling La 'Real"? "I'm ok pops". "You look shot to me, and that don't look okay". He said looking me over with a frown. "Besides being shot, I'm a smoking gun," I said with a smile.

I was wondering who called him and looked at my wife, and got the wink meaning she did it... So, I gave her that I'ma get you face. "So, who's doing Bryant "BQ" Quintell's funeral"? Pops asked me. For a minute I had forgot about my dude being dead. "Angie wanted you to do it pops", Shontay said. "I'll do it, but it's gonna be a lot of media, being the officers didn't follow procedures of a warning shot before shooting". "What"? I asked him from the bed. "It's been on the news all day, along with the shooting that left one in the hospital and bullets in parked cars and houses... You wouldn't happen to know who that could have been, do you"? "Nope". I answered. "Excuse my language pops," Stix said "those crackers is crazy as fuck". Pops looked at me. "Life don't come back when you lose it in the flesh, only the soul". "This is a wakeup call, when the Lord is speaking and wanna be heard". "This don't have nothing to do with a color code, this is life and death...spiritual and flesh thang". "I hear and know the meaning of yo words".

He smiled, bent down, and hugged me. "Can we cut the late-night gun battles out"? I may be a preacher, but I was hood before I found my lane". "As a father, I would be willing to give my life, please don't change my belief". He said and walked out the hospital room.

"Damn bro, you gonna bring the ghetto out in the preacher"! Sissy said laughing. "Shut up Sissy. He was already ghetto before I brought it out in him" Pops became pops to everybody, being that none of us but Shontay had a dad.

Chapter 18 – Dis Song Is Dedicated to the Homies

BQ's funeral was more like an assembly. I believe over a thousand-people showed up; hood vets, to sets, to pimps, to hustlas, to media, to police and the rest was friends and family. I was seated in the front row with Angie, the kids, his mom Francis and all the rest of the "We All We Got" organization. The sermon that pops preached was beautiful, all sinners have a future through Jesus Christ. I was still sore, plus I had the nasty shit bag on, YUCK. I hated the bitch ass nigga Classic. Everything went peaches, until the viewing happened to bring in a face we all didn't wanna see. I tapped Stix and pointed at Dynasty. "Look who had the nerve to show up"! "Hell naw, she out of pocket"! She walked up to the casket, and I had noticed her stomach when she got closer.

She looked in and kissed him on the forehead and mouth. I heard Sissy cough and get up and follow Dynasty to the door.

Everybody was going to see BQ for the last time and it was our turn to say goodbye.

BQ had killed for the family and would forever be our lil brother. Tank kissed his forehead and stood back. Hasko set a pair of gloves in the casket and kissed his forehead. Raw hugged him in the casket and kissed his forehead, Stix walked up, put his cellphone in the casket and whispered in BQ's ear, that he will always be a call away and kissed his forehead. BJ slid a pint of Hen in the casket by his hand, and said, "this is for when you see me again, we can drink together" and kissed his forehead. Last, but not least, it was me. I dropped to my knee, said a prayer, stood up and put my head on his chest. I reached in my pocket and grabbed a picture of him and Stink. I put it in his hand along with the replica of tanks chain, "We All We Got", and kissed him on the forehead. Before I walked away looked around and found the funeral director in the corner. I walked over and told him, "You see all the shit my people put in that casket"? "It better still be there when he go in the ground" and walked away before he could respond.

We were the last, but when Angie got up there she

flipped out. "No, no, no Bryant, no, please! I'm sorry baby, I love you"! She said, kissing him on the lips. "No baby, please don't be mad and leave me like this"! Hasko got up and grabbed ahold of her, and we all surrounded and hugged her. "No"! she screamed, "No, please Lord, not Bryant" For the first time since his death and my shooting, I think she realized the truth . . . he was gone.

I knew she wasn't high, because she seemed like she had just found out for the first time. BQ's mom grabbed her and walked away from her son comforting Angie. BJ had paid for the casket and it had all our names stitched in, with a photo of his kids, Angie, and his mom. The funeral was nice, but it was too early for my nigga to be gone. At the burial ground we all threw dirt and basically buried our own brother. (R.I.P. BQ AND STINK)

On the way out, we were stopped by Dynasty, Sissy and Shontay. "How's everything"? Besides why we are all here". Dynasty asked as we walked up. She looked different and not just because she was pregnant. Nobody spoke" ... I know how y'all feel about me already and I don't blame y'all". "But the fact is I'm pregnant with his child". She said rubbing her stomach. "How you know it's my niggas baby"? Hasko

asked her. "When I do business, I keep it clean". Here she

said, handing Hasko the date of her conception. It read the day Tank called my phone with the bullshit. "So, what you want us to do"? I asked her, speaking for the first time. "Be an uncle like you are for the rest of his kids and accept mine like you do the others". "'He who is without sin, cast the first stone", I quoted from the Bible. Sissy looked at me, and Shontay looked at me. I looked at Dynasty and said, "If you're being real about the baby, that's most definitely family. "I can do what you asked". "No matter how bad I disliked what you did, everybody makes mistakes".

"I'm not the same person I used to be". "I now own my own salon and my real name is Deseray Parks, I don't go by Dynasty anymore...not since meeting the two of them". She said pointing at Sissy and Stix. "They could have taken my life, but they gave me an opportunity to live and I wrote Bryant and told him about his child and apologized"! She went in her pocket and took out her cell phone. "See, here's the numbers he used to call me from". We all looked, pulled our phones out and matched the number that was in her phone to ours. "Yep". Tank spoke up. "If he forgave you, how can we hold a grudge"? My name is Tee, Deseray". He said holding his hand out. Stix said, "you already know me and my wife

Sonya". "Legendary and my wife Shontell", I said. "K. O". Hasko said. "JB" BJ said. Finally, Raw said, "my name is Paul". "Glad to meet you all...when the baby is born Sonya will know. She has my number". "Okay, we gone stay in touch". I said grabbing my wife's hand. "I text everybody for the after gig at the church". I needed to eat and change the shit bag.

(EVEN IN DEATH, BQ WAS FULL OF SURPRISES. I LOVED AND ACCEPTED HIM, RIGHT ORWRONG, AND HE FOREVER WILL BE OUR BROTHER... BQ MADE THE LAST RIDE COUNT)

Chapter 19 – Da Champ Is Back

I had stayed out the streets after BQ's funeral because I needed to heal from the wounds, plus I didn't trust the bitch ass nigga Classic . . . especially if he felt like I felt.

It had been a month a half since the shooting and my

shit bag had been removed a week ago. When I first took a shit, it felt like I had shit out a pumpkin, my ass was so sore. Shontay left her building to come home and tease me. I had been an "in the house daddy", for the twins and they were getting big and spoiled. Crawling everywhere and putting everything in they mouth. "Baby", Shontay called out when she came in the house. "Huh"? I yelled back to her. "Yo boo boo okay, da poor baby". I did my sad face and shook my head no. "Aww, you want me to kiss it for you"? She said in her, baby I'ma fix it voice. "No babe, it's okay". "Good, because I ain't into lickin ass"! "Shut up". I said, and she laughed. "You ready to get out and about"? "I'm good" ... "Why you say that"? "Babe, this the longest, you ever been in the house". "I love my family, plus I had to heal, and you've been raping me". "How can you rape the horny and willing"? She said laughing. "Okay, taking advantage of me". "Please, dats my dick". She had come a long way, from insecurities to acknowledging she was the best that ever did it. Her Legacy Village was a hit, in the Community and she, Mrs. Sykes, was the queen in her line of work and in my heart. I didn't make Shontay this way, I just gave her my belief.

Her and Keisha became friends and she understands why I picked Keisha to be the manager of the Legions. I'm proud of Shontay. She allowed the insecurities to be washed and flushed down the drain with all the dirt. A man cannot allow his heart to bleed water, when its blood embedded in the relationship. A house is bigger than its appearance. Empty shadows can fill a house with nightmares, instead of dreams.

"Where's my princess at"? I said knowing that it was four hours until she needed to be picked up. "You know where she's at, you dropped her off". Shontay said back. "I know" ... "Aye babe, I think I'm ready to put out a new CD". "What you been writing about"? "The Godliness in life and all that surrounds happiness". "Babe, you been had the gift to uplift the block to a building". "Why sit on the gift you been given?

"When you told me, you rapped years ago; I couldn't tell because sometimes you love the craft, then you don't'. "If it makes you happy, take it over like you did with the dope game". "Make love to the booth and bring the real love back to what you share with the streets". "You really gas baby, and I've always been yo number one fan". "Whenever you ready, I'm here to listen and support you". "I'm not just the wife/baby mama, I'm the best friend and yo battery when you're drained". "Are you happy in what you have"? "Yes, I am very happy, and I wouldn't take shit back"! I said. "Enjoy yo hobby baby and perfect the craft". "I respect yo business". She said kissing me. "I love having such intellectual everything in you". I told her. La 'Real Jr. crawled over and made a noise. "Dis boy is either attached to you, or he don't want you kissing me".

"You kissed me". I said kissing her back, and LJ flipped out. "I think he's nuts about us both". "Or just nuts"! We both laughed. "I came home to give you some nookie, and to see if the champ still existed, but dat boy ain't going for it. . ..and I ain't got no panties on"! "Why"? "I wanted you to watch me play with it before you take over" ... "Let me smell," She dipped her hand in her pussy and wiped the juice on my mouth and nose. "I'm ready and by the look of yo boxers, you are also". "I'ma put him to sleep". "Can I meet you somewhere"? "Nope, you gotta take it later now". She said getting up allowing her pants to drop and putting her pussy in my face as she walked by. "I'ma stick this in every hole"! I called after her. "It's been a while, but we will see" ... "I'm going to lay down naked".

Shontell was falling asleep, so I made LJ a bottle in which he finally went to sleep 20 minutes later. I popped up at my room door, and Shontay had the vibrator on her phone and had it pressed against her pussy. "Come get this pussy champ". She told me. I laid down next to her and played with my dick, for her amusement. She tried to grab it, but I pushed her hand away. "No". I told her. "Please babe, I'm soaked" I rubbed some juice off her pussy and put it on my dick and began to stroke it. "It feels like I could cum just watching you". She said breathing hard. "If you put it in now, you can start back there".

"You want it bad, huh"? "Yes daddy, real bad". "Please let me feel it"! I reached over and put some juice on her ass from her pussy. "I'm ready, please daddy". I touched the clit fast, and she humped my finger. "Pretty please daddy". I told her to turn around, and she did. I rubbed my dick on her pussy, and heard it talk from the juices. "You hear her daddy"? "She beggin to feel you". I slipped my dick inside her pussy, all the way and whispered in her ear, "you want the champ"? "Yes". She said trying to pump me. I banged her pussy, 15 deep and fast strokes. "Oww, the champ is here"! I banged 15 pumps, grinding motion. I could see the cum; 10 deep, 15 grinding, 4 snakes, and took my dick almost out the pussy and plunged 3 in and out. "Shit, aww fuck baby". I took it all the way out and pushed it in her ass fast. "I'm cummin" ... she moaned. I reached around and grabbed the button. Then rammed my dick deep in her ass, "AWW babe, I'm cumming hard". I snaked, and she lost her breath. I was still playing with her button and cum came out her ass. Then I stuck my dick deep in the pussy with a monster bang. Pumped snake, plunger, fast pumps, and it exploded. Shontay passed out...literally, and her cum squirted everywhere.

I stopped and went down and licked her pussy til she woke up bucking and fucking my face, "What is happening baby"? "I can't see...it feels too good". I sucked the clit soft and stuck my fingers inside of her to reach her G-Spot. She came more than, I've ever seen her cum. Then I put my dick back inside and slow stroked her until I came, busting inside her. She couldn't talk . . . I lay there and slapped her pussy, with my hand and watched her buck, then she started crying. "What's wrong"? I asked her. "I missed my champ...please don't get hurt again". "Girl shut up, I'm okay". "Dat was the best performance ever". "Look at my pussy I'm still cummin. You even made the ass thing feel like heaven, and I think passed out"! I started laughing, "You did pass out babe".

"What do you be doing to me and where you learn yo moves"? "The champ never needs to practice. He has home-court advantage". "I'm probably pregnant again, how you just did me". "Maybe, you want a morning after pill"? "Never, you keep doing me like that, and we will have the biggest family ever"! "I love you". "You ain't ready for another baby yet"! "No, but every time you dick me down like that I get pregnant". "Sorry"... "When you in me, it be worth it". "I'd give anything if you asked, swear". "I'ma slow down baby" and I got up to go get my princess. "Do you want me to grab two morning after pills"? "No". "I will, I love you". "On everything you da champ, I'm sleepy". "Nite-nite," I said kissing her eyes. "I'm still cummin"!

"Da champ is back" ... I said in my Muhammad Ali voice. On my way to pick up my princess, I stopped by the store for pills and to get my baby some gummy bears. In a rush, I stopped at one of the hoodest places; instead of going to one of my own establishments, Fast Trip, on MLK. I stepped out the white Q45, with burgundy leather interior sitting on Lexani 22's. When I touched the store, it was a few chicks and niggas I knew, but either they stuck up or they on they own program. I waved and kept moving towards what I was in there for. I'm standing behind a female, who I couldn't see her face until she turned around and it was Angie. "Hey Legend, how you doing"? She said looking nervous. I didn't answer because she had the appearance of a goblin. Her face was sunk in, her eyes glazed and big as saucers, with a busted lip and pipe blisters. "Wassup Angie"? I said. "Nothing haven't seen nor heard from anybody since the funeral".

"Yeah, everybody been on ice trying to keep a low profile" ... It was my turn in line, so I excused myself, "excuse me Angie". "How you doin today buddy"? The clerk asked me with a mid-eastern accent, sounding like Abu from the Simpsons. "I'm doing okay, and yoself"? "I'm doing good buddy, very, very good buddy" "That's great to hear...umm, can you give me some of them gummy bears and two morning after pills"? "Man, buddy, I never see guys take them buddy". That will be $15.70, buddy". I laughed and said, "me either buddy", pulling out a $20 bill. He hit the total and gave me my change, "thank you, come again".

"Have a nice day". I said walking out. When I turned Angie was gone. I went to get in my ride and saw a black glass house, bout a '72, pull on the side of me. The window came down and I knew then where Angie had went. She was in the car with the bitch ass nigga Classic. "Hey, um, bro"? "Do you know where I can get a 4 1/2 hinge of snowflake"? Angie asked me. The question caught me off guard, because I was busy staring across her at the bitch ass nigga Classic, sitting in the driver seat with a .45 in his lap. "Naw, I don't deal candy sis". "I'ma honest business man". The whole time, my eyes never left the bitch ass nigga Classics. I thought to myself, why would Angie ask me a dumb question like that?...

Then it clicked! She was trying to give, the bitch ass nigga Classic a close up on what I looked like again. "Really"?

I jumped in my Q45 and went to pick up my oldest daughter. When I got there, she was outside playing. "Hi ma'am, I'm La 'Real Sykes and I'm here to pick up Eni'yah Sykes". "I believe she is outside, but please give me a second and I will get her for you".

"Okay". She called over the radio, "pick up for Eni'yah Sykes". Seconds went by and you heard another voice, "affirmative, we're on our way". "10-4" It was like four minutes, then I heard, "daddy". I turned around and had to catch her in my arms, "hey princess, you ready to go"? "Daddy, I was playing outside with my friends". I thanked the teachers, who smiled at me. Me and my daughter are headed for the door, "do you wanna stay here"? "No daddy, I wanna go with you". "Okay".

I unlocked my car doors, put her in her seat belt and got in. "Here, I have yo favorite". I said passing her the gummy bears that got from Abu. "Gummy bears"! She screamed. "Yep". "Thank you, daddy"! "How did you know"? "I'm the king, member"? She nodded her head, smacking her lips eating the gummy bears. When we pulled off from her school, I noticed the glass house behind us. FUCK! I picked up my phone and called Stix. "Hello"? he answered. "Aye bro, why the bitch ass nigga Classic behind me and I got my daughter with me"? "Where y'all at"? "I'm on Freemont and 15th". "What is he in, and do you got a firecracker"? "He in a black '72 glasshouse, tints and 22's... and yeah I'm thunder cat".

"I'm in the sage green Navi, and when you see me hit the block and keep going"! "Aye, he got Angie in the car with him so be cool". "I'ma see what's up". "Daddy, I like the yellow ones". Eni'yah said from the backseat. "Give me one". I said staring in my rearview. She reached over and put it in my mouth. "Thank you, baby". "Welcome daddy". She said putting the headphones back on, to the TV she was watching. "Aye bro, you see me"? "I'm the fifth car behind you". I heard Stix say into the phone. "Yep". I said, twisting the corner. The glasshouse hit the same block and then the sage green Navi.

Having both cars by half a block, I hit another corner. "Bro, I'm on them". Stix said calmly. I'm hoping my daughter couldn't hear him. I heard a cannon open, POP POP POP POP POP POP, then metal and glass, then rubber. "Bro"? I said into the phone. "Yeah"? Stix answered. "Who was that getting off like that"? "Dat was me bro and Angie ain't in the car". "It's him and some niggas"! "How you know"? "Because, there isn't no windows in that joint, and they got back at me"! "Are you on the freeway"? "Yep, where you at"? "In chase. ... think I touched something in that car"! "Let that go, and I'll meet you at Dialers beach, at the restaurant after take my baby home". "Yep," "Thanks my nigga"! "Any time, for my bro and my niece".

Inside I was mad as fuck, because the nerve of this bitch ass nigga. With me and my daughter in the car. Somebody had to pay for fucking with my family, and that somebody can be anybody who cross the line. When me and princess got in the house, Shontay was up and moving. The twins were looking to escape, they play pen.

"Aye champ, what's wrong"? She said flipping a burger. "Nothing, why you ask that"? "Because yo left eye is slanted, and you are gritting a little bit". "Oh, dats my gloat face". "Babe, be for real". "How you know, how to do me like that"? "I'm yo husband Shontay, I know every inch of yo body and what it needs"! "Oh, because for some reason you know some shit I ain't used to, I swear...and like it". "Bruce Lee was my sensei" I said moving my lips like a Chinese movie. "The touch of death". "Here go yo pills," I said reaching in my pocket. "Really"? "Yes, really". "Until you're ready". "I'm always ready". "I mean smart ready, not horny ready". "I'm not taking

197

them"! "It's up to you, last time you came like that we made twins, so gather it's three after what happened today". "I think you might be right". She said, grabbing the pills, and putting them in her mouth. "We pick the time for the next child together, deal"? "Deal". I said, kissing her on the eye-lids. She smiled. "Babe, put me up a plate, I gotta meet Stix". "I was cooking for my champ and kids". She said with a pout on her face. "I will be back to eat". I said and kissed her mouth. "Be safe please, because you still got that angry look on yo face"! "Okay" . . .

I traded the Q45, for my '81 Regal out the garage. When I looked up Shontay was standing at the door. "Why you changing cars from new to old"? She wanted to know. "I need to rest that joint, don't need people knowing my whips". "Be careful La 'Real and come home in one piece"! "Okay". I said and drove off. My phone buzzed, and it was a text from Shontay, "I love you more than life La 'Real and I didn't take the pill" ... "I'm always ready when it comes to the champ". She crazy, I thought to myself. I called Hasko and asked that he meet us down at the spot.

Pulling up I saw Tank, Hasko and Stix. "Damn Legend, I got married with y'all bro". "What, I can't ride with y'all now"? Tank said. "All day long my nigga". "I just wanted the data first". I told him. "Well, even if you ain't got it, call me for the lift". Tank said back. "Yep...wassup y'all"? I said, hugging all my niggas. "Shit". Hasko said. "Wassup wit my guys"? "Who hungry"? I asked. Nobody spoke. "Where y'all wanna go converse"? "The beach is cool". Stix Said. "Damn bro, Shontay had to know something was wrong". "You in an '81 Regal and you own a car lot". Tank said laughing. "She did, but I ain't pillow talk". "She still nervous from the last time".

We walked to the beach. Hasko lit a cigarette and looked up and said, "aye Legend, why the nigga Relly 5.0 remind me of yours"? "Really, I was hoping you could tell me the same thing". "What'chu mean"? "My shit was stolen and if yo cousin got my whip... who stole it"? My eyes turned into those of an angry person. "Not me my nigga, I'd never bite the hand that fed my family". "So, I hope you ain't insinuating such a thing bro"!

"Nothing bout the Legend, is subliminal nigga"! "If I shoot my shot, you would know, because I'ma say just that"! "Aye, y'all niggas, need to calm that ol bullshit down". "Member we are family". Stix said looking at both of us. "That's bro's 5.0 the nigga got, but we don't know how Relly got that shit". "It being yo cousin, you may need to find out"! "I'm on that Stix. On BQ". "Now let's get back to the business, we came to talk about". Tank said. "Yep," I said back. "What happen bro"? Tank wanted to know.

I seen the bitch ass nigga, and Angie at Fast Trip today. Angie rolled down her window and asked me where she could get a 4 1/2 from, like I sell dope still". "Where was the nigga at"? Tank asked me. "In the driver seat, .45 in view for me to see". "He probably didn't remember, what you looked like, and had her ask that question so he could see you". Stix suggested. "Dats what I was thinking also Stix, to myself". "Then when I went to pick up my daughter, they were behind us". "Like they were watching you"? Tank frowned. "Yeah, I called bro and he got them niggas off me". "Did Eni'yah know, what was going on"? Stix said looking grim. "Nah bro, she was tuned in to the Disney tape she got".

"Classic...Classic... I think that cat fuck with Snake and Relly tough like". Hasko said. "Black glasshouse, chrome wheels, glass packs"? I asked him. "Yep, that's the one". Hasko flipped his phone open and put his finger to his lips. All we could hear was, his side of the convo "aye, what's up cousin"? "Why you ain't hit me"? "Yeah, everybody on the paper trail". "We need to hook up and smoke something" ... "At auntie Eva's". "Yeah, give me 20 minutes...yep". Hasko hung up the phone and said, "I'ma get on that now Legend".

"My bad for the snap earlier". "I see how and why, you would think that, but I'd die for my niggas before I turn Judas, "We All We Got'. I hugged him and told him my bad too. "When you get something, hit our phones". Tank said.

We jumped in the Regal and slid by Angie's house. We ain't see the car, so I dropped them back off to they whips and went home. Hasko went to his aunt's house and Relly and the nigga Snake was there. "What's up relative"? "What you into"? Relly asked him. "Shit, out and about looking for the pot of gold". "Who got that fire tho"? Hasko said back. "Boy, you know I keep that". Aunty Eva said. "Yeah, you do that aunty". I said, "what's up with you though Relly"? "Starships and rockets cousin, ready for the Matrix". "What was yo one potna's name you introduced me to a few months back"? "Who"? "The two Cats"

"Who Relly"? "La 'Real and Jamie"? Aunt Eva asked her son. "No mom, that wasn't they names"! "The Legend nigga". Snake said. "Oh, my nigga rap". "He out the way, but what's up with him"? "Dat nigga tow my nigga Classic off this afternoon"! "Legend"? "Yep, dats the nigga I got the 5.0 from". "His uncle Magnify gave account of his mama house and Stonez, his dead brother, having hundreds of thousands in the spot stashed". "So, Magnify gave y'all a map on my niggas house"? "Naw, he was down 30 racks, and was paying rent for fucking with kids in the pimp game. He told me everything".

"I'm the nigga, who went and snatched the whip and all the other shit". Snake said smiling. Hasko smiled, because he had never liked the Snake nigga and knew he just ran the stop sign. "Why y'all telling me all this shit and you know I fuck with Legend tough"? "Because whoever shot my little brother today, gone get it". "We don't die, we remain active". "Remember yo boy Stink"? Snake said with a wink. I knew my aunt was in the house, so I smiled and got up to leave. "Aye Hasko," Relly said, "blood is thicker than water and our moms is sisters". "Don't forget yo bloodline relative". "I hear you cousin". "Oh, and any blood of mine who can allow a snake nigga to speak, and rattle words about my dead and gone nigga, in my aunty house, can sleep with the fishes, cause his nut sack is too small to be respected". I walked out the door, and Snake followed me and said like a snake hissing, "Hasko, Sssseeee you later," and winked again.

When Hasko called me, it was after 10. "Aye, Legend. Me, Stix and Tank is almost to yo house". "It's that bad"? I said looking at Shontay sleep, and all our kids in the bed.

"Yep". "Okay, text my phone, when y'all get here". Hadn't none of my potnas, knew where my new house was but Stix, so it had to be bad and he had to trust Hasko's word to bring them here. I grabbed the 40, with the 30-round slab and went downstairs.

Shontay came down one minute later and asked, "why you leave yo family in bed"? I have to meet Stix, Hasko and Tank outside". "Here"? "Yes". "Is everything okay baby"?

Knowing she only asked because nobody but Stix and Sissy had been out here, "No, it's not. But please don't worry". Shocked that I had told the truth, she came and hugged me. Feeling the gun on my waist she asked, "are we in danger"? "Not y'all, as in our family, no but earlier picking up Eniyah, the bitch ass nigga Classic followed us, and it got ugly".

I could see the tears in her eyes, "He was acting tough, with our daughter in the car"? "Yes". Just then the text came in. "Okay, be safe baby. love you". She said and then backed away from me. I looked at her and walked out, "I'll only be outside baby". "K".

I got in the car and looked at the faces and could tell that God would have to forgive us... or call us home. "What's up"? I asked them getting in the car. "Aye my nig, yo uncle Magnify got you robbed from in jail, talking about what yo grandma's house held inside". "He was in there paying rent, for the pimp shit and got 30 thousand in debt, gambling". "Classic is

hooked up with Relly, Snake and whoever you shot today".
Hasko told me. "Shot today"? "Yeah, Snake say you shot his
brother today".

I knew I hadn't even busted my gun, and that Stix was
the shooter, but I wasn't gone say so. "Snake and a few of his
potnas, hit yo house for Relly's money yo uncle owed and
came across the 5.0 and the other shit". "So, Magnify told
these niggas bout my family, knowing it was my house now"?
"Yep, and the Snake nigga made reference to killing Stink".
"Damn! "Them niggas knew you were gonna tell me, and they
did so as if they wanted war... or they don't give a fuck"! "I
want Snake". Hasko said, "And how the Relly nigga, allowed
ol boy to jump out there in my aunt's house, he severed the
blood between us". "Meaning what"? Stix asked. "He can get
it too my nigga"!

I sat for a minute, then asked, "Is everybody money right
in this car"? Nobody spoke up, so I did, "I'ma give you a
hundred racks Hasko, and a hundred for you Tank. Take that
and get some land somewhere out of this town because it's
about to rain. Move your families out, by the end of the week
and I'm ready"! Tank spoke up, "I'm with you bro". "Wait here
and I'll be right back". I walked in the house, and Shontay
was right there.

"Hey". She said. "Hey". I said back but kept walking and went upstairs and she followed me. "That bad, huh"? "Yep, that bad". I said, reaching for 200 racks. "Will you tell me what I need to do, if anything at all?" "Yes, I will." I said closing the wall, behind the wall. "I will speak with you in a minute." Please pour us both a drink, stiff.

I walked back outside and got back in the car and handed Tank and Hasko they money. "Today is Tuesday they 20th, be ready by the 28th. I got out the car and never look back. I went in the house and explained to Shontay, I needed her to have some of her employees run all her businesses. I told her to buy us some property in the country, somewhere with no neighbors. "We will be gone for six months, but we are gonna keep this house." I told her my uncle was the one behind our house being robbed and the bitch ass nigga Classic, was back in the picture.

In the middle of talking Sissy called, Jamie had apparently told her about Magnify. She was mad as fuck. "Sissy get yo bidness in order and in six months we will be back." "Do you have somebody who can run the houses gig?" I asked her. "Yes bro, Yasmine". "Okay start looking for a house next to ours, out in the county." "Where?" Norfolk, VA, Texas, Arkansas, Mississippi, Kansas, or Oklahoma. Shontay try to put us close together. "Ok bro, I'ma go on the computer now. " "8 days, is yo money, right?" "Nigga, they ain't stop making money when you started gettin it"!!! "Right, I feel you sis."

"Tell Shontay, we going to Virginia"! "Okay, get some sleep". "Hell naw, eight days is fast"! I laughed, "I love you Sissy". "I love you too, but we need to figure something out for Magnify also"! I called and got all my businesses straight. I left my cleanup man Crysis, in charge of the apartments, I yet allowed Keisha to run them. I called the lawyer Ray Dupree and left him to handle the rest of my shit. I called my dad and asked him could he hold 7 duffle bags for me. He asked what was in them, and I told him cash. He asked how much, and I told him, "4 million". "Boy, you almost made me lose my godliness". "Where you get all that from"? "Was that you, who put that money in the church when y'all came"? "Yes pops, and I got it from saving since was 15 years old". "I'ma hide it in the church". "Okay". "Wait, where are you going"? "What's going on"? "A whole lot of prayer". "Ok, say no more". He said back.

Chapter 20 – Payback Is A Bitch

My whole family relocated for today, and now it was time to get to business. Hasko's people went to Kentucky, Tank's went to Texas. We called BJ and Raw to get everything done right. The whole crew was back together, including a few new ones. Relly was the first to get crept on. He's a flamboyant, type of cat who needs attention . . . especially from a female. So, we sent in a known hitter.

Relly was in the club throwing money away, on the bruised body strippers. When out the corner of his eye, he seen a Clydesdale with the body of a goddess. She walked by him and he grabbed her hand. "Aye baby girl, passing me ain't winning the race. ... I'm the finish line". "What do we win"? She asked him. "A brand-new car". He told her. She laughed at the Bob Barker, but came back with, "maybe driving ain't my sport...maybe I just like to ride"! She dropped dat ass and gave emphasis on her meaning.

"Fuck a wheel, I need a lasso for that wild thang"! "You like to be saddled or bareback"? She stood up and whispered in his ear. "Both make me buck, but I like to get beat and stretch my legs out before the derby ends".

"Damn baby girl, you shifting my pants and you ain't even touch me". "What's yo name and destination"? "Silky, but you can call me Seabiscuit for this race". "He loves the way I ride it"! She dropped it and made the ass clap. "I'm going over there to get a drink cowboy". She laughed. He got up and threw a hundred-dollar bills on the bar. "Get whatever she wants to drink". "Thank you," she said to him and turned to the bartender. "Can I get two double Remy's and a beer back"? "Coming right up beautiful". "My name is Relly, Stallion". "I'm the mayor of Portland, without the election". She reached out her hand for him to shake. "Glad to meet you handsome"! "Here's yo drinks ma'am". The bartender cut in. She licked her lips and thanked the bartender, then turned to Relly. "Are you going to tip the nice man"? Relly threw a 20 and smiled, "of course I am". The bartender was one of

Crysis' old potnas, and knew she was coming. "I ordered one for you too". "Are you gonna have a drink with me"? Crysis potna had spiked the one on the left, and the one on the right was flat pop. She couldn't drink being that she was currently still breast-feeding, her son of two and a half months. "Yeah, I'm drinking". He said grabbing the drink she gave him. Stallion picked her drink up and she canceled the whole thing in one drink, slapping the cup on the table. "That's all I need to get me started for the whole night". Relly downed his, then grabbed her hand and asked her to ride with him. She got in his 5.0 with the Gucci seats in that joint and asked to be taken to the nearest motel. "I wanna feel something hot inside me".

He drove two blocks and made it to the Motel 6. When they got in the room she stripped butt naked and watched that he did the same thing. "Let me dance for you before you fuck this pussy". She started playing with her pussy and he lay in the bed and nodded off quickly. She turned her back and the tattoo of Clack was no longer there. It was a new one that said "R.I.P. BQ "WE ALL WE GOT".

She called us, we were already close. She had a rental in the parking lot under a Jane Doe. "Good looking Dynasty". I said hugging BQ baby mama. "Deseray, but anything for my family". "I'm a woman of my word". She said and walked out the room. We wore wigs and gloves, knowing forensics would be here. Stix pulled out a needle of raw tar, while I scattered drugs around the room. He injected a full syringe in Relly's vein guaranteeing to kill him and get the coroner high. Then we left . . . leaving the 5.0, he can't drive it in hell.

The next on the list was the Snake man himself. We had to be slicker than a snail to get the reptile. He was at a hood function with three of his goons. Two of which, was the two little niggas Stix and I shot on two different episodes. I had shot the little nigga from the barbecue coming out my house and Stix had shot the other one, who was in the car with the bitch ass nigga Classic the other day when they followed me from my daughter's school. The other car was unknown, yet still a loud mouth like the rest of the pack.

Snake was in the function promoting gang bangin at its finest; red belt, red shoes, and green everything else. You would have thought the nigga was a Christmas ornament of some sort.

"Unthank livin, blood", he yelled against the beat. The party was live, big drink, powder on plates, weed and major bitches. The music was so loud you couldn't hear screams and yells...shit, you couldn't even hear gun fire. An unknown nigga ran by Snake bumping him. Alcohol went flying all over his brand-new outfit and in his face. "Nigga, on Unthank Park, dat nigga got me fucked up"! "On Bloods"! The nigga who bumped him kept running as he never noticed that he just spilled all the shit on a nigga who wasn't with the bullshit.

Now in high pursuit, of the nigga who slid by on a disrespectful note, Snake and his three homies were moving fast through the crowd trying to catch up with this nigga ASAP like. The nigga who bumped Snake went out a side door in which led to a dark path, and Snake and his goons followed. "Aye blood," Snake yelled, feeling it big and mad. "You bumped me in their homie and ain't said excuse me or nothing...as if the Snake a busta of some sort" ... "Aye you" ... The runner stopped as if he didn't have anywhere to go and went to a bush like he had to piss. "Aye nigga, you hear me blood"? Snake said walking closer to the runner. When he was three feet away, Hasko turned around and took his hoody off. "Yessssss Snake, I heard you clearly". Hasko said and winked.

"O, this bitch ass nigga! It's you who bumped into me like that huh"? "Member, you said you would ssseee me later"? "I decided tonight's yo last time seeing anything". Hasko started to laugh like he told a joke. "You don't decide bitch ass nigga"! "I decided Stinks' fate and I'm for sure gone decide yours". "You hear this nigga blood"? When he turned to look at his homies, he looked at Raw, Tank and BJ, who had guns to the little niggas heads. Hasko walked up to Snake and pulled out what he held in his hand when he faked like he was finna piss in the bushes. "Neva turn yo back on a snake... he might bite you". BOOM! and blew his brains every which way. From there, his potnas joined the serpent and tough guy who talked too much, which ended up getting him and those with him burnt.

Sissy caught her walking down the block, high as an elevator. . . "Hey, is that Angie"? "Girl, how you been"? "Who is that"? "Sissy"? "Yeah girl, where you going"? "Just walking around thinking... you know BQ's mom took the kids until I get better"! "What's wrong with you to where you ain't got yo kids girl"? "Ever since that shit with yo brother at my house and BQ's death, I've been kinda messing around with the smoke thing". "Really"? Sissy asked. "Yep, but I'ma bounce back". "Watch"! "Aye, my brother told me you were looking for a 4 1/2 pack...you and ummm" . . . She said snapping her fingers.

"Classic"? Angie asked her. "Yeah, y'all find it"? "We didn't want no work girl. He was just trying to see Legend"!

"For real? How did he know where, my niece went to school at"? "When we was in the car, I kinda slipped and let the cat out the bag". "Member, my kids went to that spot for a minute". "Right" ... Sissy said walking closer to where Angie was. "My brother and family treated you an yo kids like family". "We even paid for yo baby dads funeral and paid yo rent, and you repay us by trying to get my brother killed and his daughter too"? "No, it wasn't like that Sissy". "It just kinda slipped out my mouth and then he dropped me off". "Here, hold this"! Sissy said, stabbing Angie in the chest. "You been dead, since the crack took over". Sissy stabbed her five more times, to make sure she didn't make it. "My sis died with BQ...as well as the love".

I had seen Classic in the same glasshouse, in which Stix shot up and the windows were now fixed. He drove down Commercial a few times, I followed him to his house with some fat bitch. He must of went and fucked because I was outside in the cut for a good lil minute waiting for him. All the time he was in there, I thought about how he was gonna try and kill me with my daughter in the car. "Daddy, I like the yellow ones", Eni'yah had said. So innocent, not even aware of what harm she faced... Was this nigga gone kill her and me?

A tear dropped from my eye, and I slid under his vehicle. At first my vision was blurred, just thinking about how innocent kids and others die every year from careless niggas like this one, by gun fire. Who can turn a good woman, into a clucked-out crack fiend. Who would sell her mama out, for the next hit and pawn her kids' whole existence to take flight. I wasn't the monster, he was, and somebody had to mate this pawn.

He came out talking on his phone. "Aye my nigga, I need some more of that fire. . . Nah, I'm just coming from an in and out spot... A thick white chick, super dome control" Sniff, Sniff. "I've been out of commission; some nigga shot my windows out when I was looking for the nigga who shot me" ... "I had the nigga and his little punk ass daughter". "On the set, I was gone end the niggas thoughts". He was standing near the car and opened the door and sat halfway in and halfway out the car. "I'ma get the bitch ass nigga. I'm Classic, know what I'm talkin bout"? I knocked up under the car. (Thump, Thump) but he kept talking. "Give me like a week, and I'ma knock em down". I knocked again, because he must not have heard the first time. (Thump! Thump) "Hold on my nig, something under my whip". He got out and got on his knees to look under the car, but as soon as seen his eyes I put the 40 to his head and pulled the trigger. BOOM!

I jumped from under the car, "bitch ass nigga, you can't try and knock a nigga off with his family around" ... "'When you meet Satan, tell that nigga I said Legend sent you"! I pulled the trigger four more times, and left holes in that bitch ass nigga. I could hear the caller yelling hello, but the only one Classic would see and hear wouldn't be on this end. I had to save the best for last, being... what type of family nigga send cats to a dog's house. My uncle Magnify.

Magnify had been on drugs heavy in Sheridan and in debt. He woke up to go to yard as he did every day. Something seemed different about today because when he got out the cell, everybody was quiet but stared a lot. He wondered why the yard seemed so hushed, when this yard was the place of gossip and everybody knew everybody business. He went to breakfast and he seen niggas whispering and staring. When he left the chow hall to go back to his cell, Big Modal from Cali intercepted him, "Aye Magnify, let me holla at you"! "What's up Modal"? "Aye, you seen them pictures"? "Pictures of who"? Magnify asked. They walked to his cell and he was pulled in. "What's going on y'all"?

"Aye," Modal said to Spank and Bank, two niggas who was waiting in the cell. "He like to rape and beat on lil girls," he told them throwing down pictures of two 13-year-old girls Magnify had beat and shaved them bald. "How y'all get them pictures"? "Don't worry about the pictures bitch"! He said greasing up, "I'ma show you how them kids felt, when you did that to them". They grabbed Magnify and raped him, to within an inch of his life. I hear they call him Maggie now, like my grandma. He full-fledged gay now.

Six months passed out the way and everybody made it in the clear. We believed, being nothing had come back to us. When we came back to Portland everything had changed. I mean, I went to check on my business, only to find out everything was plus. My apartments had been ran and kept clean by Keisha. She was the best candidate for the job and I was happy I hired her.

I pulled up in the newest edition Lex bubble, and called Keisha outside. She came outside and met me at the curb. "Hey," She said smiling, "long time, no see". "How you been"? "Hey," I said. "I'm glad while I was gone, you really handled yo business". "I knew I could count on you". "I told you I was qualified for the job". "Do you have the keys to the Audi on you"? "Yes, I do". "Why you need them"? "I'ma need to use yo car for a few hours". "What about the Lexus"? "I'm pretty sure you wanna drive yo own car" ...

She screamed and hugged me. "Thank you La 'Real"!

"Thank you, Keisha". "In the glove compartment you will find a check for 10 thousand, also my wife said to give her a call if you need help starting yo own business". "We got yo back". She cried and hugged me again, then pushed me aside and ran to the car.

Yasmine ran Sissy Real Estate Company, like it was hers and made good investments. She did so well, that they added her as a partner, so now it's five of us. If you didn't guess, let me tell you Shontay is five and half months pregnant. She never took the pill and, yes, it's from that session. We never heard about what happen when we made our fast exit, but Hasko did come back for Relly's funeral. His aunt Eva thinks he had something to do with it, but its suspicion only. Tank stayed where him and his family relocated to, as well as the others involved. BQ's mom was given 40 thousand, in the mail, for the kids and a house by Sissy for her and her grandkids. We loved Angie, yet she had been destroyed by the demon on her back. So, we took care of the kids. Dynasty became a part of the family, and she fuck with the chicks in our family tough. . . (We All We Got Family is Everything) ...

Preface from "We All We Need" . . . (We All We Need. A Judas Amongst Us)

It ain't no such thing as a perfect World, nor ending to a story. So, allow me room to clear my throat and the misunderstandings. Me and the organization I had created was supposed to ride off into the sunset, and remain stable for whenever the rain fell, but all that glitters ain't gold. Meaning the Huxtables live in the 80's and the perfect family is impossible to have in this white man's world. Shit is constantly hot on my block. It never fails to be guns shots. . .

Breakfast time, upper tier fuck, I hated waking up to reality, knowing my few mistakes could cost me my life in prison. I was currently incarcerated for a spree of murders and a drug conspiracy, charging me with being the brain behind the death of Speakerbox, a federal informant, the bitch ass nigga Classic and the Relly cat, with suspicion of more.

What was read to me verbatim in the court room was that I persuaded BQ to manipulate info, from a prostitute named Barbie, and that he had told her of me being a drug dealer and the one with the contract on Speakerbox head, to set free

Raw, and furthering my criminal empire.

Then we have a mister Robert Carter, who went to the grand jury on me concerning the murder of his friend Classic. Robert States that he was on the phone when Classic was killed and heard me talking to the dead man's body as I continued to shoot him repeatedly.

Then, my uncle Magnify, not only turned into a faggot but also the police tipster. He figured out who sent the pictures and linked Relly's murder to me from the 5.0 being found in the parking lot of the motel. (Even though the car wasn't in my name, it was registered in my uncle Stonez in the past, so that connected me to the car).

After returning from the trip, I made the move and took Keisha the brand-new Lex bubble and I got into her Audi. I slid out the parking lot of the Legions and was surrounded by dozens of undercover officers at gunpoint. The first officer to approach me while I was cuffed was from the cold case unit, named Leonard. "Hey Sykes, I've been waiting on yo arrival for quite some time now"! They picked me up off the ground and put me in the back of a Suburban 1500. "Look buddy, we're not gonna play pity patty with you now". "We know everything, so hopefully you will make it easier on yourself and shed some light on the situation". Leonard said.

I laid back in the seat and just closed my eyes. I thought back about the happy times with my family, and who would be hurt most about my situation. Shontay, Sissy, Stix, and the rest of my niggas... the kids? A tear dropped from my eye, but I never once talked to the people. (I don't speak Pig-Latin!) and I knew I faced crucifixion. The only person who could clear me of these charges, was with God... Jesus.

None of my family members were indicted with me. There was nobody to point a finger at none of them, yet the police kept they eyes peeled on everybody that had dealings with me.

THE BEGINNING, OF THE END

Eddie Ray Strickland Jr.

Out of the Northeast side of Portland. Fresh out the Fed's on the appeal of 15 years, to a book writer. The loss of my brother held me down for so long, that I couldn't see past the streets and focus on becoming a better man for my family and friends... With this being positive, I strive to be the best man I am capable of being mature like... I have sacrificed so much to turn back, and I thank God for this talent. I am 39 years of age with the thoughts of bigger things to come. I dedicate this hard-earned work to those I lost on the way and pray that on this journey I'm able to touch many. Thank you for your time and look me up for the wave of more books to come. (ADRUM)

From the Author's Desk....

Today's youth are growing up fatherless, and we as a

community of color need to stay together and fight against

violence. By no means are the ways of people in this book mine, nor am I glorifying the hood life that I've lived. I've lost too much as a man, to go back to being a kid at mind. "I would like for the world to read and feel my pain, as I reach to become a better me".

I was sentenced to 15 years for having guns and living life off the flash of a gun, instead of using my thoughts and intelligence. "The pen is mightier than the sword". If you expect something different in life, from what you grew up involved in, then you must change the belief, that you'll fail and add the accomplishments that come from being positive. I would like to say, "I'm here to stay but, I'm not gonna count my chickens before they hatch".

In the hood they say that everything ends the same; death or imprisonment. Some may move away to outlive the gossip and hatred in the hood. There's a 70% chance that the way you grew up, while in the hood will determine your whereabouts after the hood.

Let me know where I'm at (with this book), and look for the books "We all We need", "A Judas Amongst the Crowd" and "Destiny".

"We are hard-pressed on every side, yet not crushed; we are perplexed, but not in despair; Persecuted, but not forsaken; struck down, but not destroyed" II CORINTHIANS 4:8-9